PRAISE FOR THE 5 C'S

"I have known Dr. Mitra for nearly thirty years. There are few individuals I know who have had such a positive impact on the community in which they live. Dr. Mitra's work ethic and positive approach to life demonstrates that you can be successful in the workplace and simultaneously enrich and strengthen your community as well. His book, The 5 C's, reflecting his life's amazing story, offers valuable ideas for entrepreneurs and leaders to succeed."

—TIMOTHY P. MURRAY, PRESIDENT AND CEO OF THE WORCESTER REGIONAL CHAMBER OF COMMERCE, FORMER LIEUTENANT GOVERNOR OF MASSACHUSETTS AND FORMER MAYOR OF WORCESTER, MASSACHUSETTS

"Dr. Mitra reflects successful entrepreneurship, true leadership, and unselfish philanthropy. He has had a proven track record as a Rotary leader. It strikes me that he is clearly a person of action who both talks the talk and walks the walk. No doubt his skill as a motivational speaker played a significant part in his achievements. His book offers very simple yet very powerful ideas, making it a must-read for entrepreneurs and leaders. The inspirational, real-life story makes it very readable."

—KR RAVINDRAN, PRESIDENT, ROTARY INTERNATIONAL, 2015–16

"The 5 C's is steeped in rich culture with strong supporting family values that ultimately define an entrepreneur's success. This book takes you on a journey from a mud shack in India to a high-rise in Worcester, Massachusetts. It's a must-read about turning the pains of life into satisfying success."

—CRAIG L. BLAIS, PRESIDENT AND CEO, BUSINESS DEVELOPMENT CORPORATION

"Dr. Mitra is a well-respected community leader and entrepreneur whose book is irresistibly inspiring."

—CONGRESSMAN JIM MCGOVERN, MASSACHUSETTS, 2ND DISTRICT

"Starting off life in difficult circumstances, finding himself homeless for a time, and yet achieving remarkable success, Dr. Mitra is now head of an extremely successful tax and financial services company. He has earned a national reputation as an entrepreneur with novel ideas who has given back not only to various charities, but by providing personal guidance to young men and women on how to start and succeed in business. Dr. Mitra's new book, The 5 C's, is an American tale of how hard work, education and the support of family helped him to succeed in his quest to be an entrepreneur. His book is a remarkable 'how to' for any entrepreneur looking for inspiration and guidelines to follow."

—FRANK CARROLL, FOUNDER AND CHAIRMAN, SMALL BUSINESS SERVICE BUREAU, INC.

"*Dr. Mitra's unforgettable life experiences mold his perspectives on leadership, opportunity, and success. This book is different because Dr. Mitra is different. Whether you're a start-up or an established entrepreneur, this book will be a very pleasant and uncommon asset to your business journey.*"

—KEVIN MACILVANE, VP, DIVISIONAL SALES MANAGER,
BRIGHTHOUSE FINANCIAL

"*Satya Mitra's new book, The 5 C's, is the perfect encapsulation of both his own personal experience and the true American story of hard work, dedication and community service; all characteristics that have distinguished his success as a remarkable leader and successful entrepreneur. I expect to recommend The 5 C's to students who seek advice on what will aid them in being successful as leaders and professionals—and to be happy in doing so!*"

—BARRY M. MALONEY, PRESIDENT,
WORCESTER STATE UNIVERSITY

"*I have had the honor and pleasure of knowing Dr. Satya Mitra since arriving in Worcester three years ago. He is an invaluable partner and advocate for our great city. Dr. Mitra is a tireless community and civic volunteer, leader, family man and above all a great friend. His book, The 5 C's, offers unique ideas not commonly found in business publications. I believe Dr. Mitra's lifetime of experiences provide entrepreneurs and leaders the secret to success.*"

—PAUL PROVOST, PRESIDENT,
WORCESTER TELEGRAM & GAZETTE

"*Satya Mitra is a natural leader with a proven record of success and a leader who inspires people to perform their best. It has been my privilege and honor to observe Satya's leading the Worcester Rotary Club to one of its largest membership growths in its 100-year-old history and collecting record amounts of monies. He has spoken and has been acclaimed at countless Rotary clubs throughout the world and has raised a large donation of money for the Rotary International Service Foundation. In my opinion, Satya will succeed in anything he undertakes.*"

—ROGER W. FROST, DISTRICT GOVERNOR, ROTARY INTERNATIONAL, DISTRICT 7910 (1995-1996)

"*Satya Mitra's true spirit of giving and commitment to others shines through in this inspirational story of heartache and challenges that would bring most to their knees. But it is his story of 'rising up' and his entrepreneurial success that are profoundly inspirational. Geared to business leaders and young people alike, The 5 C's details how to harness passion, creativity, and desire into an entrepreneurial spirit that is strengthened by giving back to the community and by supporting others. This is our imperative for educating students at the college level—to be innovative as they develop their authentic selves so they can find meaning and purpose in all that they do.*"

—NANCY P. CRIMMIN, ED.D., PRESIDENT, BECKER COLLEGE

"Satya Mitra's personal journey from the depths of poverty in India to successful businessman and philanthropist in Massachusetts is a moving and inspirational story. The 5 C's is an engaging book, full of thoughtful and helpful ideas to help readers become more compassionate and successful in their business and personal lives and transformative leaders in their communities."

—GEORGE TETLER, PARTNER,
BOWDITCH & DEWEY, LLP

"Satya Mitra is the embodiment of the American success story. An immigrant from India who knew poverty and hardship firsthand, he always had a deep appreciation for the sacrifices others made to help him along his journey. Today, he's dedicated his life to sharing the core principles and values that helped him achieve his goals, and his book, The 5 C's, can help any reader find real meaning in their success."

—PETER STANTON, CEO AND PUBLISHER,
WORCESTER BUSINESS JOURNAL

THE 5 C's

THE

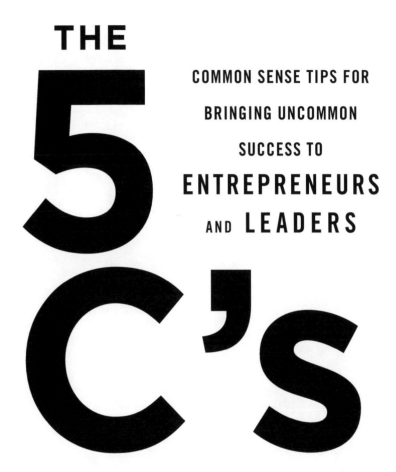

5
C'S

COMMON SENSE TIPS FOR BRINGING UNCOMMON SUCCESS TO **ENTREPRENEURS** AND **LEADERS**

HOW THE CHALLENGES OF LIFE BRING POSITIVITY TO EARN SUCCESS

DR. SATYA MITRA, PHD, EA, CFP®

LIONCREST
PUBLISHING

THE 5 C'S

Common Sense Tips for Bringing Uncommon
Success to Entrepreneurs and Leaders

ISBN   978-1-5445-1346-1 *Hardcover*

978-1-5445-1344-7 *Paperback*

978-1-5445-1345-4 *Ebook*

I sincerely dedicate this book in loving memory of my Ma (Mother), Babu (Father), and Gurudeb (Priest).

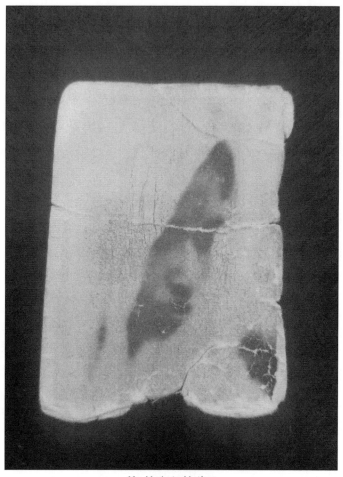

_Ma_, My Late Mother

Ma, I do not remember you. You brought me to this world and left me very early. But you left me with a purpose to help and be there for others in need. The picture of you I always carry, the only picture of you ever taken, is how I recognize you. I always feel you within me. Stay with me, Ma.

Babu, My Late Father

Babu, you raised me with the love of both a mother and a father. You sacrificed your entire life for me. You sowed the seeds of entrepreneurship, leadership, and public speaking within me. You are my biggest motivator; your words of wisdom are the foundations of my life and success. Babu, I hear your words every day. Keep talking to me.

Guru, Our Family Priest

Gurudeb, my family and I are so fortunate to have you in our lives.
My profound faith in your blessings made me an entrepreneur. I
would not have changed my profession if you had not instructed
me. You inspired me to share the success with the community.
You gave me the directions to life. You are my navigator. May
your blessings continue to shower upon us. Joy Guru!

CONTENTS

INTRODUCTION

All my life, I have been chasing three dreams.

I wanted to be a successful entrepreneur.

I wanted to be a great leader in my community.

I also wanted to die happy.

But before I leave this world, I want to achieve many goals. To support my two sons. To always be there by my wife. To lead. To make positive changes in the community. To lift up those who need lifting. To make others proud of me. To give back. To write this book to inspire you to do the same.

If I can accomplish all of these goals and dreams, my last breath will spell "Satisfied." My hope is after reading this book, so will yours.

THE STRUGGLES OF TODAY'S ENTREPRENEURS

Anyone who has started a business knows the daily stress of being an entrepreneur. Feeling overwhelmed, lost, or unsure of yourself or your path. Wondering if your investment will ever pay off or if you'll ever make it in the business world. I know that struggle. When I was starting my own business, I felt that way too. There are so many "ifs" associated with being an entrepreneur, and those doubts are amplified by everyone pulling you in different directions. The struggle is enough to make you lose confidence in yourself and your dreams.

The purpose of this book is to guide you through the noise. The ideas and concepts in these pages are not the only way to find success, but they are what have brought me success as I define it. You won't find graphs, statistics, or numbers. You won't find sample business plans. This isn't an abbreviated MBA course—it's a book of lessons I've learned and strategies you can employ to harness your common sense to build an uncommon success story.

A LONG ROAD

My road has been full of both hardships and blessings. I grew up in Tirodi, a small village in India. When I was three years old, my mother contracted brain meningitis. Because we were rather poor, we couldn't seek medical treatment in time, so when she died at age thirty-two, I was left without a mother.

I was much younger than my two siblings, born twelve years after my brother and ten years after my sister. My brother had been staying with close family friends at the time of my mother's passing, and he continued to live there after—a request she'd made on her deathbed. A year after my mother passed, my sister was chosen by a groom. At fourteen, in line with tradition, she went to live with her new husband and his family.

Then, it was just me, a four-year-old boy, and my father, a heartbroken man whose own health was steadily declining. Many times, walking to and from his job as a schoolteacher, he would collapse and need to be carried home. I stayed with neighbors while he was teaching, but when he came home at night, it was just the two of us. Then, when my father was forty-two, it became clear that he could no longer continue to work due to his health issues, and he was forced to retire.

At this point, we had no income. Soon, we would have no home.

We traveled to my uncle's village and asked if we could live with their family. For a time, the arrangement worked. However, my father felt like a burden on his older brother's large family and limited resources. Eventually, we left and went to stay with another uncle, this time my father's younger brother. During this period, my father was making money however he could, often going into homes to do personal tutoring. I would walk with him to these appointments, sometimes miles away, afraid to leave his side for even a second. Even when he'd visit the bathroom, I would follow. I had already lost my mother. What if I lost my father too? On those long walks, my father would share stories and lessons, many of which I still carry to this day.

Soon, my other uncle could no longer continue to let us live with him. My father and I became homeless. Sometimes, we'd get lucky and be permitted to stay with a family my father was tutoring, but that never lasted more than a week. We were vagabonds.

Then, my brother, who had completed his education and found work as a teacher himself, began to send my father and me money. He suggested we rent a small place. We found a *jhopdi*, a term we use in India for a very small house made of mud. When it rained, the water flowed inside the tiny structure and pooled on the dirt floor, but it was better than being on the street.

Living this way was difficult, but we managed. Little did we know one of our biggest challenges was yet to come:

my father's vision deteriorated until he ultimately became completely blind. He never lost his sense of gratitude for what we had, though. Being led by my father's example is one of the many blessings I've experienced in my life.

Thanks to my brother's support, I was able to attend school. Eventually, I excelled academically and earned scholarships. My brother never got to pursue further education himself because my father and I relied on him financially, so he was determined to give me every opportunity available. He helped me earn my undergraduate degree, my graduate degree, and eventually my PhD. His wife was just as generous. I am grateful to my sister-in-law, who saw how important it was for my brother to help me. I sometimes wondered if she would object, but she never wavered. After they had sons of their own, they simply treated me as an older son. My sister, too, supported me even though she'd married young, sharing a strength and selflessness that has always reminded me of my mother.

My family priest, or Guru, was another incredible blessing. After I came to America, my PhD in biochemistry in hand and eager to pursue a career in biomedical research, he advised me to change my course, to become a full-time tax consultant and help the community. I was devoted to my Guru and believed wholly in his wisdom. Thanks to his direction, I've been able to build a successful business that not only supports us, but also supports my employees and their families. That business, The Guru Tax and Financial Services, has grown from the ground up and stays true to my Guru's teaching of using the business to help others.

RISING UP

My wife and I started our tax and financial planning business in our basement in 1990. We started with no clients or income, but with lots of confidence and faith. Today, The Guru Tax and Financial Services works with over five hundred clients in twenty-six states and many different countries. I am also one of the top producing investment advisors in the brokerage firm HD Vest Financial Services. I am pleased with my business success, but I am most proud to have never laid off any of my employees and to have given them yearly raises, even during tough economic times.

As my Guru told me many years ago, business success must be accompanied with serving the community. I believe I've always served the people in my community well. I'm highly active in my city of Worcester, Massachusetts. I've received the key to the city from the mayor, and I'm the recipient of an Action Hero Award—an honor given for helping the community. I also currently serve on ten local boards. As a former President of the Worcester Rotary Club and as a Rotary Club Assistant District Governor, I have twice been honored as Rotarian of the Year by the District. I am also the founder of a nonprofit foundation, Joy Guru Humanitarian Services, that gives back to the community in a variety of ways.

This is what success looks like to me—moving from a mud shack to a classroom to a basement office to a high-rise office building. Watching my two sons receive degrees from Duke, Harvard, and UPenn, and go on to pursue their dreams—one is a lawyer and the other a standup comedian. Knowing my wife, Sheema, is always by my side, I could not do what I've done in my life without her. In good times or bad times, she's always there, jumping in with a smile to cheer me up or celebrate. Even as I'm writing this book today, she is the coauthor—not only of this book, but my entire success story. Her support is unbelievable.

I have risen up and found meaning in my life—an amazing outcome because after my mother died when I was three years old, I often wondered why I was even here. Why did she have me so many years after my brother and sister? I knew I was an unplanned child, so what was my purpose?

I now know that there was meaning in my mother's passing, but I didn't always understand it, especially as a young child. On the day I saw my mother's body being taken from the hospital in Nagpur, I noticed everyone was crying. I turned to my sister.

"Where are they taking Ma?" I asked.

She didn't want to tell me what happened since I was only three years old.

"Mother, she has been so sick," my sister said. "She's going to a bigger hospital in heaven. When she is better, she'll be back."

From that day on, every time I heard a plane flying above, I would run into my front yard, hoping the plane would land and my mother would step out. I ran and I waited. I ran and I waited. My sister and other family members never told me to stop. They thought that with time, I would grasp the reality that no plane was coming—and eventually I did.

To this day, I believe my mother did land. She landed inside my heart. I carry her picture with me all the time, the only picture of her ever taken. I don't wonder about my purpose any longer. I know she left me because she knew I would have to feel pain myself in order to know and address the pain in others.

My mother was always helping someone else. Doing

more whenever she could. Reaching out her hands. Now that she's landed within me, I hear her whispering in my ears, "Son, God took me to relieve me from my pain, but I left you behind so you can be there to heal the pain of others." So, Sheema and I strive to do that. That is our purpose. In this book, I'll describe what I've learned along my journey and share The 5 C's so that you may get one step closer to finding your purpose as well.

MY HUMBLE GIFT TO YOU: THE 5 C'S

My life experience has left me with a unique perspective. I want to share the wisdom I've gathered in building a successful, long-term business and becoming a leader in the community. My toolkit for success contains five tools I call **"The 5 C's": Connect, Communicate, Create, Confidence, and Contribute.** I'll explore each concept in depth in these pages, but taken together, here's what they do: they help you understand and use your passion and imagination to propel forward your business—and your life.

The 5 C's will teach you how to grow your business and how to maintain that growth. They will show you how to take ownership—a favorite lesson from my father. Today, when I complete a tax return for a client, my father's words echo in my mind. "This is my tax return," I think. "How can I best finish the job?" Whether you're the owner of a business or the leader of a community group or both, The 5 C's will help you understand the value of taking complete ownership over whatever you do.

The 5 C's will also help you understand how to not only lead your employees, but how to win their hearts in the process. You want your people to work with joy in their hearts and smiles on their faces. That starts by inspiring them to take ownership of their work just as you do with yours—and appreciating and rewarding them when they do.

Ultimately, The 5 C's will demonstrate that your true success as an entrepreneur comes when you give back to the community and touch another life. That is the purpose of my business and everything I do—to not just be happy with myself, but to be happy seeing that my business stands in the community as a source of hope, dignity, and support for those who need it. The following pages will detail The 5 C's not only to help you become a successful entrepreneur, but also so that when you look back on your life one day, you too will be able to say that you are "Satisfied."

CHAPTER ONE

GIVE:
BUILD THE FOUNDATION OF PROSPERITY

"This life is short, the vanities of the world are transient, but they alone live who live for others."

—SWAMI VIVEKANANDA,
SPIRITUAL LEADER AND PHILOSOPHER

Before we dive into The 5 C's, let's begin by establishing where we are going. The ultimate goal, for me, is to not only build a successful business but also to share that success with the community. Your achievements can help people and touch lives. Based on my experience, every entrepreneur will be successful if they aim to give back to the community. Giving is the river that runs through all that you do.

The desire to give back inspired me to write this book. While part of my goal here is to convey an entrepreneurial success story that you might emulate, the overarching theme is giving back. When you've finished this book, I hope you will have new tools to achieve success in your entrepreneurial or leadership role, but I also hope you will appreciate that true success comes when you bring a smile to the faces of people who are in need of help or have lost hope. Following The 5 C's will allow you to become a giver, closing the loop of true achievement.

THE GIFT OF A LIFETIME

Between my mother's death, my father's illness, and our poverty and homelessness, my childhood was difficult. Nonetheless, I was fortunate to go to the reputable Central Drug Research Institute in Lucknow, India, to earn my PhD in biochemistry. The typical trajectory for graduate students at that institution was to complete a degree and then continue studies in the United States; the professors had attended American universities and could help students with connections.

That path, however, was not my dream. My father was sick, and my primary focus was staying with him and showing him that even though he was blind and paralyzed, he was not alone. I wanted to give him a good end to his life.

Destiny, though, had other plans for me. I truly believe that my transition to America was divinely orchestrated.

One day toward the end of my program, while I was still living in the dorm, I received a letter. It was an offer letter for a postdoctoral position at the University of Louisville School of Medicine in Kentucky—a research position in the department of obstetrics and gynecology. I had already opened it and started reading when I realized the letter wasn't meant for me. It had been intended for another student who had already found a position and left for the United States.

I told the story to one of my professors, Dr. C. R. Krishnamurthy, the Head of the Department of Biochemistry and asked him what I should do with the letter. He asked, "Well, why don't you apply for the position?" The other student had already graduated, but he believed I would qualify as well and would benefit from continuing my studies in the United States. I explained that I didn't have the money to travel that far and wanted to stay close to home to help my father. But my professor insisted. It would be better for my father if I advanced my education and then returned home, he said, rather than turning down such an important opportunity.

I had great respect for my professor; out of reverence, I could not say no. I took Dr. Krishnamurthy's advice and wrote to the University of Louisville, telling them that the person they had written to had already found a position but that my professor suggested I apply. I enclosed my résumé.

Within two weeks, I received an unexpected response: the university officials offered me the position! They provided the necessary documents for me to get a visa. I told my professor that I had gotten the position, but I didn't feel I was truly eligible to go since I had not finished my dissertation yet. He said that he believed I had done enough to merit my doctorate. He told me to wrap up what I had completed and he would recommend to the university that I be awarded my degree. I was not convinced, but—again—I did as he said and presented my work to the committee. The committee ultimately found my research novel enough to warrant awarding my doctorate early.

Dr. Krishnamurthy told me to go to the U.S. Consulate in Delhi to apply for my visa. I went to submit my application along with five other students from my graduate program. At that time, it was difficult to get visas approved. We were applying for what is known as an exchange visa, which allows a person to enter the United States to work for a designated period of time before ultimately returning to his home country. Part of the application process is meeting with an official in the Consulate's office and persuading them that you will, indeed, return once your study is complete.

All five of my classmates had their interviews before I did. And all five were rejected. They didn't make a compelling enough case that they wouldn't overstay their visas. I assumed I would be rejected too, which would have been fine with me, as I wanted to stay with my father and didn't have the money for the trip anyway. My brother was paying for my schooling at the time, and I couldn't ask him to pay for my travel too. Still, out of respect for my professor, I went through with the interview.

In my meeting with the consulate general, he explained that many students had arrived in America and decided to stay.

"What guarantee can you give me that you will return to India?" he asked. "Do you have a job or property to come back to?"

"No," I explained. "I do not have a job or property to return to, but I will definitely be back because my father is very ill."

"Many applicants speak of sick relatives but end up overstaying their visas anyway," he continued. "What other assurance can you give me?"

"I'm willing to sign a bond that says when my visa expires, I can be deported back to India," I said. There wasn't actually such a form for me to sign, but he must have been moved by my willingness to put my assurance in writing. To my surprise, he approved my application.

I now had a visa and no money to travel. I wondered what I would do next.

I walked into a small travel agency to gather information and spoke to the owner. I asked him, "How much would it cost to fly from Delhi to New York City and then to Louisville, Kentucky?" adding, "I am just trying to find out the cost, but I don't think I can go."

"Why are you thinking of going?" he wondered.

"I just received a visa for a postdoctoral fellowship, but I don't believe I have the money to go," I explained. "I just want to know how much I would have needed."

"You're going to further your education?" he asked.

"Yes," I said.

"Well then, you're going," he said. "I am going to pay for your travel."

Shocked, I asked, "You're going to make such a kind gesture when you don't even know me?"

"I know you enough," he replied. "If you're going for your education, I would like to help you. This is a loan, not a gift. Once you're established and earning money, you can repay the loan to my brother-in-law who lives in New Jersey."

I couldn't believe someone who had just met me would pay his success forward and help me achieve my dream. It seemed like divine intervention. When I told my brother and my father what had happened, they both wanted me to go—they would be so proud for me to be the first in the family to study in America. My father told me not to worry about him and that we could be together when I returned.

If not for the travel agent, I would probably still be in India today, but coming to America started me on an immensely successful and fruitful journey. I've learned so much and had so many opportunities in this country. Ultimately, I fulfilled my promise and repaid the man's brother-in-law in New Jersey.

The travel agent may have thought he was just giving me a loan, but he was giving me insight into my deeper purpose. His act of kindness lit a fire in me. I knew if God ever gave me the opportunity to help someone else, that is what I would do. The experience helped define my mission in life: to empathize with others' difficulties and to use my success to step forward and help. Empathy allowed me to come to the United States, and I brought it with me to give to others.

THE CULTURE OF GIVING

Growing up in poverty, I depended on the mercy of others. That charity came mostly from family rather than people in the community. In my experience, because of limited resources, India does not have the same culture of giving that America does. The travel agent was certainly an exception and he changed my life. One of the great gifts of coming to America has been witnessing the generosity of the people here. People go to church regularly and give money as an offering, or they see victims of a natural disaster or other catastrophe and immediately feel moved to help. Americans face hardships and difficulties, but part of the greatness of this country is that giving is sewn into the minds and hearts of the people from childhood. It's a place unlike anywhere else in the world.

When I was a child, I didn't think about giving because I had nothing material to give. Once I got to America and witnessed the innate culture of giving, though, I began to consider what I could contribute. From the moment the travel agent helped me, I started a journey toward philanthropy and service to those who are less fortunate.

REALIZING OUR POTENTIAL TO HELP OTHERS

Realizing the potential of giving back takes commitment and practice. Too often, people allow excuses or issues of convenience to create barriers to generosity. While I realize we all have varying resources and levels of material success, most of us are privileged compared to a large percentage of the world's population. Yes, we have expenses related to our homes and businesses that we must attend to, but it's also essential to give back.

There are people in the world right now who have no food on their tables or roofs over their heads. We all have enough to contribute something to help those who are less fortunate. I faced many hardships growing up, so the difficult experiences of others are never far from my mind. But regardless of our childhood experience, we can all build generosity into our lives; we can make sharing our successes habitual and non-negotiable.

For example, I used to do taxes for a couple who primarily did janitorial work and earned a combined income of $30,000 per year. Even though this income was modest, they still donated $5,000 per year to their church. Each year, I saw the same thing, and it intrigued me. Though they earned relatively little, they contributed almost 20 percent of what they made. Finally, I asked them about it. They said that they lived as if they made only $25,000 per year and set aside the remaining $5,000 for those who were less fortunate. Though they were not wealthy by many people's standards, they knew they had a much better quality of life than much of the world's population and felt it was essential to give back.

This couple is an example of tremendous discipline. Too many of us procrastinate, thinking we have to get our own affairs in order before we can help anyone else. We all have many expenses, and without discipline and commitment, it might never seem like the right time to give back. If a couple making $30,000 can live as if they made $25,000 and share the rest, you could likely also begin contributing to those in need right now. I believe we should think of those in need every day, because there are so many people in dire straits. No matter how much or how little we make, we can give a portion of what we have and help them.

Sometimes people ask of charity, "What's in it for me?" or "What will I get back from it?" I believe those questions are misguided. Charity isn't a purchase; you aren't contributing money so that you can receive something material in return. Instead, it is a different kind of winning—you are paying your success forward and sharing your prosperity to bring a smile to the face of someone who needs it. Even donating ten dollars makes a difference, but first, you must cultivate the mindset of considering the needs of others.

I suggest that you don't think about what you're giving up by donating. If the stock market goes down and we have to sell, we absorb that loss. If my car has a problem and the mechanic tells me that the repair is $500, I pay that amount. We find ways to cover the costs of the things that are necessary and important to us. It should be the same with giving. If we plan for and prioritize resources for philanthropy, then giving becomes doable and automatic, just as we automatically spend for any other important reason. You don't have to give $5,000 of a $30,000 income, but you can set aside something.

It can be easy to hesitate to give when you're going through difficulties, but I believe true giving is contributing even when it's difficult. Even if you are experiencing pain, you can still share through that pain in order to help someone whose life is even harder. If you don't push through, there will always be a reason not to give or a difficulty to use as an excuse to wait to be generous until another time. It's a form of procrastination.

I've heard about veterans who have lost limbs but still climb mountains as a part of fundraisers for other veterans. They trek through snow and harsh conditions on prosthetic limbs. Why do they do it? Why go through the hardship? They understand the importance of giving back, and they've prioritized helping those even less fortunate than they are. They experienced difficulty but still persevered in their giving and found immense satisfaction.

When life is challenging, you can still give if you have the heart for it. There will always be excuses, but when we stop procrastinating or putting up barriers, generosity can become an integral and rewarding part of our lives. Often, philanthropy is what is missing from our true success.

GANDHI'S EXAMPLE

I remember hearing a story about Mahatma Gandhi. When he was trying to bring freedom to India through principles of nonviolence, he held a procession to raise funds. He was so beloved that many called him *Bapuji*, or "father figure." During this procession, he sat on a stage with his treasurer, and supporters filed past, giving him what they could. Some gave one hundred rupees, and others gave thousands. In each case, he blessed them, handed the money to the treasurer, and said, "Thank you."

Then, an old, thin woman came up to him. She carried a gnarled branch from a tree as a cane. She was clearly poor.

Although she was frail and trembled when she walked, she'd waited in line like all the rest. The woman handed Gandhi a single *paisa*—an Indian penny. He blessed and thanked her, and then he held the penny to himself.

"Bapuji, you didn't give me the penny that the old lady gave you," the treasurer said, puzzled.

"No," Gandhi said, "I'm going to keep it with me because it's very special."

"Why is that penny so special?" the treasurer asked. "Other people have given you 10,000 rupees."

"Because that's all she had," Gandhi said. "She gave everything for the cause."

Generosity lies in the richness of your heart, not the richness of your bank account. Some people are materially wealthy but still don't have the heart to give. The old woman in the story led by her example. She heeded the call of her leader and gave to the cause without worrying about her own life. Her action perfectly illustrates what is at the heart of giving despite difficulty; Gandhi saw the selflessness of her generosity and recognized that her gift was the most special one he received.

THE RIPPLE EFFECT

Someone in the travel agent's life must have shown him the value of sharing success with others. He then paid it forward and had a tremendous impact on my life. Now, I look to continue the chain of giving back and inspiring others to do the same.

Not only does giving have an impact on those who receive your generosity, but it also positively affects your own family and sets an example for your children. From watching my example, my sons are both givers. My younger son is a comedian. About five years ago, he participated as a rookie in the Boston Comedy Festival. My wife and I were visiting India at the time, and we didn't know he was one of only ninety-five comedians to be selected from 1,400 entrants. He spent the week competing against the others for a $10,000 grand prize.

Since he was new to the competition, many other comedians were favored to win, but my son ended up receiving the prize! When he went up on stage to accept his monetary prize, he explained that he felt his success as a comic came as a direct result of the support of the Boston community, so he wanted to give back to that community by donating half the prize—$5,000—to the Boston One Fund for victims of the marathon bombing that year.

He went further. Still on stage, he said that of the ninety-five comics who competed that week, he was the only one to get paid. My son told the crowd comedy was more fun when everyone gets paid, so he would share the remaining $5,000 with his ninety-four colleagues from the competition.

When we returned from India, he showed me a *Boston Globe* article that said, "The Boston Comedy Festival winner's generosity is no joke." Though he won $10,000, he went home with only about fifty dollars because he felt moved to share his winnings with others. Hearing the story made me cry.

"Son, you are my hero," I told him. And it's still true today.

Seeing your values in life reflected in the actions of your children is the greatest feeling. It's a source of pride and a sign of living an upstanding life. I know that the positive example of generosity I've set for my sons will be passed on in the family and continue rippling outward to help others.

My son was only twenty-seven when he won the comedy competition. Many people his age immediately would have thought about what they wanted to buy—a car, a television, new clothes—but he didn't hesitate to announce his intentions to give away the money. Even though he faced his own challenges getting started in life and his profession, he gave anyway. In doing so, he inspired all the people at the competition as well as those who read the story later.

In the same way, I hope this book will inspire you to pay your success forward and inspire others to do the same. The circle of generosity can keep expanding.

MAKE IT ROUTINE FOR YOUR BUSINESS

Philanthropy should be built into every entrepreneur's business model. While the focus should be on giving for the cause without expectation of reward, you will find that your generosity will earn you respect and leave people with a positive impression of your business.

It's not about how much you give, but about incorporating giving back as a serious part of your business' values and mission—a process that connects you to others in a meaningful way. Remember, there is no shortage of people who need help. Open yourself to empathizing with their difficulties, and then take action to come to their aid. As Mother Teresa said, "If you can't feed a hundred people, feed just one." Incorporating generosity and philanthropy into your regular routine can help bring balance to the world and make it a better place.

Making giving back a part of your routine and realizing the potential for your business to help others is true success for an entrepreneur. That is the end goal we are trying to accomplish. Now that we know where we are going, let's discuss how to get there: The 5 C's. Our journey begins in the next chapter by learning how to truly Connect.

CHAPTER TWO

CONNECT:
MAKE YOUR PRESENCE FELT

"Our success has really been based on partnership from the very beginning."

—BILL GATES,
PRINCIPAL FOUNDER OF MICROSOFT

With the help of the travel agent whose kindness changed my life, I arrived in Louisville, Kentucky in 1976 to pursue my career in biomedical research. It took a while to learn about American culture, making it difficult to connect with people. During my first few weeks in the country, I was working on the fourth floor of the Medical Dental Research Building at the University of Louisville when a man approached me to ask a question.

"Hey, man, is there any john up here?" he asked.

I had only ever heard "John" as a person's name, so in my mind, I started going through the list of people I had met thus far. I didn't know anyone named John. I could see the man was starting to get impatient and upset. He got up close to me and voiced his frustrations.

"What's the matter with you, man?" he said.

I thought maybe hearing John's last name would jog my memory, so I asked very politely, "Can you tell me John who?"

"John who?!" he exclaimed. "John—toilet, man, toilet."

I had come across so many different surnames based on trades or familiar words—Cook, Baker, Carpenter—so I started racking my brain for anyone I had met named John Toilet. One of my lab mates overheard the conversation and knew I was putting myself in danger by aggravating the man, so he came and pulled me aside. As he took me into the lab, he turned and told the man, "He's new here. He doesn't know what 'the john' means. The men's room is upstairs."

The man was still furious at that point. He looked at me, pointed, and said to my lab mate, "Teach him, man! Teach him. If he wants to live in this country, he'd better learn what 'the john' means."

My friend explained everything and taught me what the word meant, but that command stuck with me: "Teach him, man! Teach him." I understood if I wanted to live in America, I needed to learn as much as I could about the country and the culture in order to connect with people here.

LEARNING ABOUT BUSINESS

My research at the University of Louisville was progressing well, and the University wanted me to continue my work. They offered to be my sponsor so that I could become a permanent resident of the United States. Sadly, my father had passed away in 1977 and returning to India to care for him was no longer an option, so I accepted their sponsorship and continued my research in Louisville for several years.

In 1982, I moved to Worcester, Massachusetts, because I had a job opportunity there as a scientist. Though I was more familiar with American culture by the time I made this move, I faced another significant adjustment when I got to New England. Kentucky had a relaxed social atmosphere, but Massachusetts was more fast-paced. The friends I made in Worcester were always thinking and talking about business. If I met up with people socially on the weekends, they generally tried to persuade me to join them in different business ventures, such as buying real estate or investing in stocks. In an effort just to understand what my friends were talking about, I started taking business and finance classes at Worcester State College.

I found that I enjoyed the tax classes. In 1989, the same year I became a U.S. citizen, I decided to take the Internal Revenue Service's four-part Special Enrollment Exam. The exam was given nationwide, and those who passed received a federal license from the IRS to practice as an Enrolled Agent in all 50 states. Only a fraction of those who took the exam passed all four parts on the first attempt, but I was able to pass. I believe I passed because I had the blessing of my Guru, so I went to visit him to share that I had received my professional tax license. To my surprise, he suggested that I open a tax office on the side while I continued my career in science. I was a scientist without any business training, but my wife and I strongly believed in our Guru. So in 1990, while our sons were six and three years old, we opened the tax practice from the basement of our home.

The next surprise came in 1994. My Guru's guidance that year was to complete the transition away from being a scientist and to devote my life to helping people with their tax and financial concerns. At this point, while I had enjoyed the subject matter and helping others with tax issues, I never imagined running the business would become my full-time occupation. But I had my Guru's blessing and my wife's support, so I made the decision to change the entire course of my career without much hesitation. That year, I became a full-time tax and financial consultant.

I named the practice "The Guru Tax and Financial Services." My Guru told me I had his blessing to refer to him in the name so long as I used my business to help the community. Giving back was already on my mind because of the way that the generosity of others had impacted my childhood and my ability to come to America. Now, with my Guru's guidance, it became the core of my mission and a key value of my business.

Guru, Our Family Priest

LEARNING BY CONNECTING

As I opened the tax practice full time, the man from Kentucky's words still echoed in my mind: "Teach him, man! Teach him." In an effort to understand what people around me were talking about, I had gone from being a postdoctoral fellow in science to taking tax classes to starting my own business. I knew I needed to meet as many people in the community as possible so that they could learn what I had to offer. As a result, if there was an event in my community, I went. I wanted to get to know and connect with as many people around me as I could. Getting involved, connecting, and learning as much as I could about everything around me became central to my life.

Some business owners are less motivated to connect because it feels like another job to them. Many focus heavily on the core work of their business and feel that attending outside events is a burden. They believe there are other ways to get the word out about their company, such as through traditional advertising and utilizing social media.

You may worry that if you try to connect in person you'll be out of your depth, you won't know what people are talking about, or you'll make a mistake. Believe me—I understand. Coming from India, there were all kinds of words and customs that were unfamiliar to me when I arrived in America. It's scary to feel out of place. But I say: be bold! In my experience, in-person interactions are the most effective and rewarding. People who meet you personally and interact with you one-on-one will remember you more vividly and get a deeper sense of your work than if they happened to scan an advertisement for your services. Talking face-to-face and personally handing someone a business card has been much more effective than other strategies. Yes, you can use conventional advertising and other methods to spread the word about your business too, but there is no substitute for personal connection.

THE COST OF *NOT* CONNECTING

Sometimes when I tell people about how much my business has benefited from personal connections, they say they had never thought about taking that approach. I urge them to start immediately. Connection is something to cultivate from the beginning—it makes you and your company memorable and visible. If you haven't been connecting, don't wait! Start tapping into the power of personal relationships now.

You can start by joining boards in your community—a fantastic form of connection. I'm a member of the Planning Board of the City of Worcester, the Worcester Regional Chamber of Commerce, the Worcester State University Foundation, the Tower Hill Botanic Garden, the Greater Worcester Community Foundation, the Worcester County Mechanics Association for Mechanics Hall, the New England chapter of the National Speakers Association, and the Worcester Rotary Club. I'm also a Worcester Art Museum corporator and a YMCA corporator. My wife and I founded Joy Guru Humanitarian Services, and I am a board member of that organization as well.

Each board has a different mission, vision, and culture, yet each one teaches me so much. You may think that no board positions are available for you or that you don't have the right background to fill a board role, but you would be surprised how many organizations are looking for talented people and are willing to make room for the ones who are bold enough to ask. Look for organizations that align with your values, and then take the brave step of expressing your interest and ask to be notified if any opportunities become available.

And don't just sit on a board. Be actively involved. I don't take a passive role on the boards I belong to or simply try to promote my business. Instead, I take my responsibilities very seriously. I love looking at life from new angles through these organizations. For example, for the Worcester Planning Board, I consider how a new project will impact the community. For the Worcester Chamber of Commerce, I consider how to attract more companies to the city of Worcester. I feel very honored to be consulted and have the power to vote on these matters. To have gone from not understanding basic English slang to taking an active part in the workings of my American city is a blessing.

MAKING THE TIME AND THE EFFORT

The "John Toilet" incident may have inspired me to make connections once in I was in America, but I was taught the importance of engaging with my community at a much younger age. My father was a tremendous influence in my life, particularly after my mother passed away. A key lesson my father taught me was to get involved with the community around me and to be engaged with my surroundings. He always taught me not to make excuses. He told me that if I desired something, I should find a way to achieve it. "It's not the management of time. It's the management of desire. Manage your desire, and you will find time," he said. His words remain in my mind to this day and motivate me to act.

Everyone is busy, but those of us who make time to forge connections with others will see our companies grow. Saying you don't have enough time is an easy excuse that will have negative consequences in the end. We all work hard every day, but we must not fall into the trap of saying that we're too busy to take the important steps that will benefit us and others. Prioritize connecting in order to reap rewards.

I think about personal connections like getting across a river or scaling a mountain. You have to swim across; the other side won't come to you. You have to climb to the top; the peak won't come down to your level. Reaching out to people for your business is the same: most people won't come to you—instead, you need to go to them. If you need help from people, most likely they aren't going to notice that and approach you. You will need to reach out, call them, attend their conference, or find another way to get the help you need. You'll have to swim.

Today, I'm a member of ten different boards. Each one gives me the opportunity to connect with important people. You don't have to join ten boards, but make the time to participate in one or two. You'll be of service to your community and your business will benefit at the same time. People will see you doing your part and will respect that you've stepped up despite the time it takes and the other commitments you have to balance. In the end, they'll look at you as more than just a business owner—they'll see you as someone who cares.

Even if you are not on a board, you can still connect by making your presence felt. Whenever there's an event involving the city council, I try to go even though I'm not a city councilor. I meet people, shake their hands, exchange business cards, and follow up later. If there's an issue that's important to me, I make a public comment about it. In that way, I'm participating in the life of my city while also signaling to those around me that I am invested in what happens in my community.

Local television or radio appearances are another way to connect with the community. You can call up a host or station, explain what you do for a living and what kind of information you have to share, and see if they have a slot available for you. They might not, and that's okay. If you don't call, though, you definitely won't get the opportunity. If you do call, you might just find a new platform to engage with your community. I've done quite a lot of those appearances to talk about a wide range of topics. Making such an appearance automatically lends credibility to me and my business since viewers and listeners presume someone talking about a subject on TV or the radio must be an expert. Of course, it's important to reinforce this presumption by preparing thoroughly and demonstrating a solid grounding in the field.

If you truly can't get out and connect face-to-face on a regular basis, perhaps due to physical challenges, don't give up on making connections. Maybe forging new connections daily or weekly truly isn't an option for you, but you can seek out and prioritize opportunities on a monthly basis. And even if you can't go out and meet people in person, you can arrange phone calls to connect with the people in the community. Phone calls are often more effective than e-mails. If someone hears your voice and can ask you questions in real-time, they are more likely to remember you positively. Even if your opportunities to connect are limited, focus on creating meaningful personal relationships with the chances you do have. You will still reap rewards.

By making the effort to connect, you will begin to get referrals. I often see new clients who were referred to me by people I once had lunch or coffee with who remembered our personal connection. In that way, my business continues to grow and thrive through the connections I cultivate and maintain. You can have similar success if you invest the time and energy to engage with your community. People who interact with you personally and see that you are honest will feel more comfortable recommending you to others. Too many business owners assume that their businesses will grow automatically just based on the product or services they provide. Time passes, and they often realize later that they could have done much better if they'd made the effort to make more personal connections. Don't let that be you; the time to connect is now.

FINDING ROLE MODELS

In my business, I work with families on estate planning and leaving inheritances to their children. My father had no material assets to leave me, but I inherited something more valuable—his wisdom. I was fortunate to have strong, supportive role models in my father and my Guru. They shared their experience and gave me essential guidance, which continues to pay dividends to this day.

If you don't have a parent or a spiritual teacher who can guide you, you can still find role models. One of the additional benefits of connecting and developing personal relationships is that you may even find a role model right in your local community. Someone I look up to in the Worcester community is Frank Carroll. He started his life as a shoe shiner many decades ago, charging people a few pennies per shine. He worked hard, never stopped thinking creatively, and ultimately rose up. Today, he is the founder and chairman of a successful insurance company that has served small businesses in my town for over forty years.

Frank is highly community oriented and gives back mightily to the people of Worcester. As a result, he was given the city's Isaiah Thomas Award, a very distinguished recognition given yearly for exemplary community service. He's also a Korean War veteran and runs a food pantry for the poor in association with a church. Helping others is integral to his values and infused in everything he does; he's always thinking about how to make the community a better place.

Frank illustrates true success: he hasn't just achieved it for himself, but he also shares what he has with others and considers their needs. I feel so fortunate to know him personally. Like Frank, I think we should all operate with one foot in business and one in the community, because our success as entrepreneurs is in the hands of the community. Frank is my role model because he stays engaged with the world and uses what he has achieved to give back to those in greater need. He is a truly successful entrepreneur, and I hope you will try to emulate his generosity and desire to connect with the community.

CONNECTING THROUGH PERSONAL STORIES

In my office, I have a picture that shows my hand with the words, "I waited for that plane every day." As I described, when I was a small child, I believed my sister's explanation of my mother's passing: I thought that she had taken an actual plane to heaven and would come back on a plane one day. The photo sparks curiosity in people who see it. They ask me what it's about, and I tell them the story. They learn more about my story, and sometimes they are inspired to share their history as well. And soon we've made a genuine, memorable connection that isn't just about the business we have together.

The photograph that hangs in my office—one
of the ways to connect with people

Your story is likely very different, and you may not need
a photo with a message like mine. However, I encourage
you to think about ways that you can similarly spark a
personal connection with your clients. You can find methods particular to your life and situation that work for you.

The critical takeaway is the importance of building a personal connection. Find opportunities to show everyone you interact with who you are and to reveal your integrity and sincerity.

Once you Connect, the next important factor for successful entrepreneurship is being able to effectively Communicate. We'll turn to that "C" in the next chapter.

KEY LESSONS

- "Connect" is the first of The 5 C's because it's so important. Relationships are built and nurtured through connection. Connection is a powerful tool to grow your business. Don't let another day pass without tapping into that power.

- Make the time and the effort to reach out to your community—constantly find ways to engage with important community leaders. Getting yourself motivated to desire connection is essential. Manage your desire, and you will find the time.

- Follow up on the personal connections you make. These personal connections will inevitably become important sources of referrals.

- Find ways to foster memorable interactions with people. Those who have meaningful, face-to-face exchanges with you will remember you.

CHAPTER THREE

COMMUNICATE:
MAKE EMPLOYEES AND CLIENTS FEEL VALUED

"The single biggest problem in communication is the illusion that it has taken place."

—GEORGE BERNARD SHAW,
PLAYWRIGHT, CRITIC, POLITICAL ACTIVIST

My father was a very effective communicator. He was always able to use analogies and give examples to make his point clear. For his lesson on taking ownership, he used to tell me that if I were a waiter, I should deliver the customer's dinner as though it were my dinner. I should clean their table as though it were my own. That example always stuck with me. Now, when I am doing financial planning for a client, I treat it as if I am doing financial planning for my own hard-earned money.

I communicate similarly with my own sons. To teach them that they should be passionate about everything that they are involved in and to get them in the mindset of focusing on every detail, I would give the example of preparing for a theater performance. The only way the performers can be successful, I would tell them, is if they treated every rehearsal like it's the final show. Apparently, the lesson stuck. When my oldest was in eighth grade, he was selected for the varsity baseball team—the youngest player by far. I spoke to his coach after the selection, telling him I preferred that my son remain on the junior varsity team so he would get more playing time.

"No, we want him on varsity," the coach told me. "I can't explain to you the effort he showed at training camp. He played so hard every single practice. It was like he was playing in a real game. He deserves to be on varsity." I was not surprised.

How you communicate will determine how effective you are as an entrepreneur. If you can master both internal communication to employees and external communication to clients, you will set your business up for success.

COMMUNICATING WITH EMPLOYEES

Communicating with employees is critical—the most valuable asset of any company is the people that make up the organization. At first, you likely started your business alone or with a few partners—in my case, it was just my wife and I. As your venture grows, though, you will have employees who need to be invested in the success of your concept; they need to have buy-in.

It is important to win the hearts of your team members. To do that, you must have excellent communication. The number one message I am communicating to employees is the lesson from my father—ownership. I want them to feel that the company is their company. When my employees come to work, I want each one to think, "I'm entering *my* office." In our office, if an employee sees something dirty or out of place, they will straighten it up because they are invested in the impression we make. It's just a small example, but they don't say, "Oh, a janitor will deal with that later." They know that when we all pitch in to do what needs to be done, we all achieve more. This culture unfolds from constant communication encouraging my team to take ownership.

But just communicating *to* employees is not enough—two-way communication is key. You must be approachable and create an environment in which employees feel comfortable sharing their observations and ideas with you.

Some entrepreneurs fall into the trap of thinking they're the only ones who can come up with the best ideas for their business. But you do not have the monopoly on new ideas. Your employees work with you every day, and oftentimes they are closer to the day-to-day details than you are. Innovations and areas for improvement will occur to your employees, and they should be invited to share those insights with you. Yes, you have the final say, but appreciate that you may not be the only one with useful insight to give. Open communication results in great ideas circulating freely and employees feeling more valued and motivated.

In my office, we have yearly planning meetings during which I solicit input from everyone who works for me. If someone brings up a good suggestion, I give them public acknowledgment and praise, and I put that suggestion into action. They feel heard and valued, and their insights help keep the business growing and thriving.

Similarly, if you plan to make operational changes in your office, you should get input from your team members and communicate your rationale for the changes. Being the boss who makes decisions from on high and then forces those decisions on employees is not effective in the long run. Employees are more likely to feel committed to your direction if they have the opportunity to help shape it as appropriate, while recognizing that you are still in charge.

Your communication should also show that you genuinely care about your employees. For example, if any of my employees has an important family event, I always make sure we cooperate with them so that they can attend. They have a life beyond the work they do for me, and I understand, acknowledge, and support them fully as human beings. People who feel valued as friends or family rather than as workers who are simply being used for labor will give you maximum effort. With this form of communication, you build genuine, lasting relationships and increase your chances of success.

COMMUNICATING WITH CLIENTS AND CUSTOMERS

Just as we must focus on communicating with those who work with us, we must place equal emphasis on our communication with those who use our services. Clients and customers are our real bosses: we work for them. It is essential for our communication with clients to be prompt and appropriate. If you've ever been to a doctor's office and had to wait a long time to be seen or called a cable company and had to wait on hold for a long time, you understand the frustration that delay can cause. Unreasonable waits undercut clients' confidence and make them restless. Responding thoroughly—and within a reasonable timeframe—is key.

In my line of work, clients sometimes get unsettling letters from the IRS. They're told they're being audited or owe a large sum of money. If they call me—often frantic and looking for reassurance and advice—I need to get back to them within the day, and preferably within the hour. The longer I make them wait, the more their worry builds. The service I provide is informed guidance, which helps people feel calm and in control. Time is of the essence.

Additionally, being proactive in your communication is invaluable. I have clients who panic when the stock market goes down. I don't wait for them to call me. Instead, I call them. I tell them there's been a market correction, and if there's anything that needs to be done, I'll do it. Communicating in this way sends the message that they can relax because I'm on top of everything. They don't need to supervise me or give me reminders, because they know I'm paying attention to the situation and looking out for their best interests.

One of the rules I created for my office is that if we receive anything by mail, fax, or email, my secretary reviews it, determines what it is, and makes sure to contact the client to acknowledge receipt. We log that the sender has been contacted. Before a client ever feels the need to follow up with us, we want to proactively let our clients know we've received their information. We may not always be able to immediately review the information they've sent, but we're always able to immediately let them know that we're working on it. Prompt, proactive communication has become part of our brand. In fact, our clients comment on how fast and communicative we are; they know they can rely on us to call and keep them in the loop.

On the other hand, poor communication will cost you clients. Clients who feel they have to manage you and who don't know when they'll hear back from you will find someone else to provide better service. People change service providers all the time because of poor communication, so don't make the mistake of being unreliable or unresponsive. If you're busy and can't respond immediately yourself, make sure your assistant keeps the client posted.

The bottom line is that responsiveness builds trust. It shows you aren't just trying to take the client's money; you're interested in their personal well-being and treating the relationship with respect.

STAYING IN TOUCH WHILE TRAVELING

You begin to gain even more trust and loyalty if your communication skills travel with you. Whenever I am out of the office, whether I'm travelling personally or on business, each of my employees sends me an update before they leave for the day so that I'm aware of what has been happening in my absence. I take time in my hotel room, whether I'm within the country or abroad, to review the business of the day and communicate with whomever I need to. We're blessed with cell phones, internet service, and other ways to keep in touch even across vast distances, so there is no excuse to let essential communication fall through the cracks.

If you run a business but are completely unreachable during a time of crisis for a client, you run the risk of losing that client. I've never had someone say to me, "I was worried about the dip in the stock market while you were visiting Africa for ten days and not responding, so I'm taking my business elsewhere." Such failures of customer service simply don't happen in my office because I've trained my employees to serve the clients as I would. I've also implemented systems that keep me apprised of any important issues related to my clients. I can't emphasize enough how essential timely, well-informed communication is, no matter where you may be.

SERIOUS CUSTOMER SERVICE

Many years ago, I was in India when a client received a letter from the IRS. He panicked and called my office. Since we have a communication system in place, my secretary let me know about the matter as soon as possible. I asked her to send me the IRS letter so I could review it.

As it turned out, the issue was one that I routinely handled. I called the client and told him everything would be fine. I would call the IRS to take care of everything when I returned to the United States the following week.

But IRS letters stir up anxiety in people nonetheless. They wonder if the government will give them a fine, take their property, or, worse, send them to prison. I could tell my client was still extremely worried. I told my wife I was going to change my flight and go home early. I suggested she stay with the kids and return when we'd planned. When I went to change my tickets, it turned out there had been four cancellations. My wife said she would rather return with me than stay by herself, so my whole family flew home a week early—all because my client was worried about a letter.

I'm not suggesting you change personal plans every time a client has an issue or a concern. But sometimes the communication with a client just needs to be face-to-face. We have so much technology now enabling global face-to-face communication, that you may not need to fly back around the world, but you may need to navigate time zones and communicate with a client at an inconvenient time for you. This type of communication and serious customer service will pay dividends in the long run. Changing my personal plans ensured that I will keep that client for life. He saw I truly cared about his situation and was willing to go the extra mile to give him excellent service. His gratitude translates into extreme customer satisfaction and loyalty.

INFLUENCING AND INSPIRING OTHERS

As entrepreneurs, we must also use our communication skills to influence and inspire others. Often, this means pushing back against common misconceptions and expressing views contrary to popular belief. Effectively communicating when you are going against the tide requires gaining people's trust and having an unshakeable knowledge of your field. If you want to persuade people, you need to understand both the big picture and the small details, inside and out. You need to be able to describe all the products and choices available in your field, and you need to assess each client's needs in order to recommend the best option for that client.

For example, in my field, there is a common belief amongst clients that everyone should stay away from annuities. However, annuities may be right for some and may not work for others—it's purely a case-by-case analysis. If a client comes to me and wants to buy shares of a mutual fund but would be better off with an annuity, I need to be able to communicate the facts and explain why. I need to be able to speak persuasively on the options, especially when that client is coming into my office with a preconceived negative impression of annuities. That ability to influence flows from knowledge. If you don't have sufficient knowledge and grounding in your field, you won't be able to convince your client of the correct path. Continually learning and improving helps build the knowledge base that will allow you to communicate confidently and persuasively, no matter what your profession.

We've discussed how to Connect with the community and how to Communicate with employees and clients. Now let's look at how to Create a unique business in the next chapter.

KEY LESSONS

- Open, two-way communication results in employees feeling invested in the company. As they feel a greater sense of ownership, their effort and dedication increases. Employees produce better results, and your business is more likely to achieve its goals if you leverage communication properly.

- Timely communication generates a sense of reassurance and confidence in your clients or customers and helps you retain them. Poor communication loses clients—period.

- Proactive, responsive communication that recognizes your clients' needs will improve your business's reputation. People will be impressed by your prompt, personal touch. They'll remember you, recommend you, and remain loyal to your brand.

- Being a persuasive communicator in the face of popular misconceptions sets you apart and builds the trust of your clients. Doing so requires gaining a deep knowledge of your area of expertise.

CHAPTER FOUR

CREATE:
WRITE YOUR OWN STORY

"You can't use up creativity. The more you use, the more you have."

—MAYA ANGELOU,
AMERICAN POET

When I was young, my father gave me a book in my native language of Bengali, titled *Moreo Jara Roilo Beche*, which means "dead but stayed alive." In other words, there are people who have passed away but whose legacies live on through the memories of the living. The book told the stories of many great people who lived in India, from leaders and freedom fighters to writers and Nobel Prize winners, including Gandhi, former Prime Minister Jawaharlal Nehru, and poet Rabindranath Tagore. These people may be dead, but they are still living on through the memory, admiration, and gratitude of the people of India.

I began reading each story slowly, one by one, to learn about all of the great people the book described. One day, I had an eye-opening discussion with my father.

"I see you're reading *Moreo Jara Roilo Beche,*" he said. "How do you like it?"

"It's very inspirational," I said.

"Why do you think I gave you the book?" he asked me.

"You probably want me to be like one of these leaders in the future, right?" I replied.

"No, son," he said to my surprise. "I gave it to you because I wanted you to see each person in the book has a unique story and creativity all their own. You don't want to be another Gandhi. You want to be yourself, with some uniqueness in you."

My father encouraged me to figure out what I could offer the world that was different from what others had done before. The key was to recognize the importance of individual creativity—not so I could copy the creativity of others, but so I could look inward and understand how to be unique in my own right.

That conversation really resonated with me. No matter

where I went or what career I pursued, I carried my father's advice with me. I learned I could be creative like those who were "dead but stayed alive" without trying to do exactly what they had done. Thanks to this lesson, whatever I do in life, I always ask myself what I could do differently that no one else has done before.

CREATING UNIQUE SOLUTIONS FOR YOUR BUSINESS

All business owners should find a way to set themselves apart by creating something unique. Creativity is essential. Even though many entrepreneurs are naturally risk-takers and have already taken the brave step of starting a business, many fall into the trap of sticking to a standard formula for running the business. They often don't think about approaching their particular endeavor in an entirely new way. They operate their companies by just following business school case studies or trying to copy what has worked for others rather than considering what they could do to distinguish themselves. If you think in this manner, you'll get stuck. Creativity is the opposite of stagnation, and it requires courage—but it pays off.

So how do you break free of the mold and start to think creatively about operating your business? Well, in order to figure out how to run your company in a way that will distinguish you from all the others, you first need to find out what your competition is doing. For instance, when I made the transition from science to tax advising, I spoke to a range of people already in the field. As I listened to their experiences, I asked myself where there was room for improvement, and I looked for opportunities to do things differently.

You can do the same. As you speak to others in your line of work, you will get a picture of the status quo and can pinpoint ways to improve upon the core work. Creativity enters the picture when you identify how your particular strengths and interests can add something entirely your own to your practice. What can you offer that no one else offers? If you do your research and are willing to risk trying something outside the norm, you can create a niche for yourself. Your unique attributes can bring positive attention to your brand, build your reputation, and help you stand out from the crowd.

DEVELOPING MY PARTICULAR APPROACH

In observing different tax preparation business models, it was clear to me that just trying to differentiate myself from the large, national tax preparation firms would not be enough. I also needed to think creatively to set myself apart from the many other smaller tax practices in my area. I began trying to understand how most of these local practices operate. By talking to other tax accountants, I found that many of them prepared tax returns while their clients waited in the office. The clients walk in and hand over paperwork, and the tax preparers punch in the numbers, print out the forms, and send the clients on their way. Many people are happy with that kind of service; it's like going to an express oil-change shop and waiting while they service your car. You're in and out quickly. Other accountants have their clients leave for two hours and come back when the tax return is done—similar to leaving your car for a more traditional mechanic service.

I saw an opportunity to provide clients with a more thorough, individualized experience, but the key would be thinking creatively to come up with a unique approach that would appeal to clients. As I considered the existing business models, I realized that all of these accountants met with the client only once. So in my office, we made it a point to meet with each client multiple times.

Before filling out any tax forms, I sit down with each client for an interview to understand their unique personal circumstances. We discuss specific considerations for that year's tax return as well as long-term goals and potential future changes in their financial situation. Based on this initial discussion, I have better information to assign the initial preparation to the person in my office who is best qualified and suited to perform the work. After the initial preparation, a second preparer reviews the documents.

Finally, I do a review. Then, my office calls the client and arranges a follow-up meeting so I may personally explain the results.

When I meet with the client to go over the tax return, we also discuss steps they can take to plan strategically and lessen their tax liability for the following year. If they have questions after our discussion, or if their tax situation changes at any point during the year, I encourage them to call me and set up another meeting. I want the clients to know that I provide ongoing support, not just assistance during tax season. Many of my clients tell me no one has ever met with them so many times and given them such a level of advice and attention before.

My business follows this detailed, multistep process because our service is advice oriented. I don't simply want to fill out forms for my clients; I want to give them personalized guidance at tax time and all year round. After looking at other practices, I made sure that in my office, there would never be a scenario where the client sits and waits while I quickly crunch the numbers and hand back the completed forms. Because of this tailored approach, I have extremely high customer loyalty. My firm now works with clients in twenty-six different states. Most of these clients started out in Massachusetts and then moved after working with us for a while. Instead of switching to a local tax advisor, they've chosen to keep working with me because I provide such a personalized service. We've built a relationship and a connection that remains strong despite the physical distance between us.

My exact approach may not translate directly to other businesses or professions, because this approach is based on my own particular perspective. But I advise you to come up with an underlying structure that will capture your creative angle and keep you focused on your particular niche. Just as my father advised me not to imitate Gandhi, but instead to learn that each of us should be special in our own ways, so too I recommend that instead of copying my model, you realize the importance of having a distinct approach. The key is continuing to think creatively and applying that creativity to your unique situation.

PUTTING YOUR PERSONAL STAMP ON YOUR BUSINESS

If you want to stay ahead, you can never stop thinking creatively. Even aspects of your business that might seem mundane or commonplace can turn into effective ways to capture and retain clients if you think creatively. I'll give you a few examples from my business.

When most accounting firms complete tax forms for a client, they provide the client with a standard IRS envelope for mailing. The client then adds postage and mails the forms. Pretty standard process, right? Not in our office. I've tried to go the extra mile to add a truly personal touch to this final phase of the preparation process. It all starts with the very first meeting. When I speak with my clients, I don't just focus on the numbers—I also take notes on their personal interests. I might jot down that someone enjoys gardening, is a veteran, loves dogs, or plays golf. At the end of the process, when I hand over the completed forms to be mailed to the IRS, I also provide a custom-made envelope with postage provided (which is almost unheard of in the field). And the postage stamps we provide aren't just any stamps: they have pictures of the client's hobby or interests on them.

My clients are always impressed that I've taken this extra step. They might ask me how I knew what they liked or be touched that I remembered our initial conversation. They can't help but tell their friends and families about it. I create a strong connection with my existing customers while also generating a unique source of referrals—all for the price of a stamp.

We also use other creative, impactful ways to connect with clients before they even walk into our office. For instance, every employee reads the complete schedule of appointments at the beginning of each day. So if a client comes into the office, every employee who sees that client, whether in the reception area or the hallways, will greet that client by their name, even if the client is coming to the office for the first time. After the meeting, when the client walks out of the office, we offer them water, tea or coffee for the road. Many offices will offer these items to clients when they walk in, but we've found that clients appreciate the thought on the way out as well. And our personal touch does not stop when they leave the office. For example, during a rough New England winter, if there is inclement weather, we'll follow up with the clients to make sure they made it home safely. In these small ways, we're constantly striving to creatively advance our commitment to connecting with people, building relationships, and making our clients feel noticed and valued.

CREATIVELY PROMOTING YOUR UNIQUE TALENTS

You likely have multiple talents and services to offer your clients, not just the one for which they initially approached you. If you don't tell them about all your offerings, they won't know—and they may go to your competitor when they need a related service. For instance, if you run a mechanic shop and someone comes to you for engine repair, you might tell them you also do body and dent repairs. If you don't tell them, they might go to a different body shop if they get in a fender-bender. In my business, if a client comes to me for tax preparation, I tell them that I'm also licensed to provide financial planning and investment advice. If I don't tell them, they might go to a separate financial planner instead of seeking my services.

I give my clients a general explanation for why they should consider using my other services; I tell them that they will receive more effective, efficient, and tailored service if they work with one person who can oversee all the aspects of their financial life, from recommending investments to doing their taxes. I also present various concrete, creative examples to help my clients understand the value of the services I offer. For instance, I ask them how they would go about building their dream home. Would they hire one contractor to build the kitchen, a different one to build each bathroom, and another one to do the bedrooms? Or would they want one competent, skilled contractor to manage the process so the design fits together seamlessly? I tell them that the rooms of the house are like their financial portfolio. Wouldn't it be better to have one person with an overarching vision of all the financial concerns to make sure everything works together as smoothly as possible?

I might also make an analogy to educating a child. You wouldn't send your child to one school for mathematics, another for science, a third for English, and a fourth for history, would you? Instead, you want a single, high-quality school with a comprehensive curriculum that works together—and an administration that knows how your child is doing in each individual subject.

It's not bragging to discuss your other offerings. Don't hesitate to promote yourself. You're simply stating facts about what you know how to do so that your customers have all the information and can return to you for other needs in the future. But to make the experience memorable and vivid, think about different ways to creatively present your offerings so that you're not just handing out a brochure or rattling off a list of additional services you provide. Think of ways to make your specific offerings strike a chord with the client. Be bold and be creative in order to leave an impression.

NEVER STOP GENERATING NEW IDEAS

My father would often focus his lessons on two concepts: being extraordinary and being outstanding. He had a very simple explanation for these words. Being "extraordinary" requires doing that which is a little bit extra than ordinary. And being "outstanding" requires doing something that will make you stand out. He used to tell me we all have brains, but our brains are usually asleep. To wake them up, we have to give them a good stretch by continually thinking of new ideas. The more we keep thinking about the possibilities, the more creative solutions arise. And sometimes that's all it takes to be extraordinary and to be outstanding.

I'm constantly considering how I run my business and

what I could do differently. I've come up with the process for having multiple meetings with clients, the stamps, the check-in calls, etc.—I'm sure there are many other meaningful and memorable things that could be done for my clients if I put my mind to it. And I do.

When a new and unusual idea arises that is aligned with your heart, values, and conscience, be bold enough to try it. Instead of worrying that no one else has tried that idea or that it might not go over well, listen to your inner wisdom. If your creativity leads you to a new solution that resonates within your heart and follows your mission, you're likely onto something great—but you have to be brave.

Never limit yourself by being afraid of bigger or more established competitors. Every large, successful business was just getting started at one time. If they can achieve great results, so can you, as long as you continue innovating and thinking about what you can offer that is new, different, and better.

I came to America from a country with a very different culture. I even started out here in an entirely different career. Still, there was room for me to succeed because I continued to think creatively. Whatever your story is, there is room for you to succeed too. This country is great because of the opportunities it offers. People will consider not only your background but also your talents, tenacity, and willingness to rise. Create your brand, define your mission, follow your values, and be creative. If you do these things consistently and with discipline, you don't need to worry what others do or what your bigger competitors are up to. Keep thinking of new ideas to make your business extraordinary and outstanding.

Now that you're prepared to be fearless, let's talk about the next "C"—Confidence.

KEY LESSONS

- Creativity breeds uniqueness. When you distinguish yourself through your creativity, it defines your brand. Never stop developing your unique solutions.

- Understand your competition so you can think creatively and bring your own personal touch. Rather than imitating the creative actions taken by others, find what works for your niche. In this way, you'll be able to highlight your company's mission and values.

- Creativity can awe your clients and customers. Your personalized and unique innovations will stun people and make you memorable to them. They'll become loyal to your brand and tell others about the one-of-a-kind services or products you offer. By exercising creativity, you will make your business extraordinary and outstanding.

CHAPTER FIVE

CONFIDENCE:
SHOWCASE YOUR KNOWLEDGE

"One important key to success is self-confidence. An important key to self-confidence is preparation."

—ARTHUR ASHE,
AMERICAN TENNIS PLAYER

Two of my first clients, Ron and Francine, have since passed away. I miss them dearly. They'd been with me since I started my business out of my basement. We met at least once a year around tax time and often more frequently than that. I loved speaking with them. They were very joyful, jolly, humorous people—always cracking jokes.

One day, though, they came to meet with me, and Francine was serious and quiet. I asked her what was wrong, but she wouldn't tell me. Finally, Ron told me that she was upset because they had been approached by a lender who offered to refinance their mortgage at a low rate if they acted quickly. Francine wanted to meet with me to discuss the pros and cons, but Ron felt that they shouldn't miss the opportunity, so he persuaded her to sign the documents.

"She's angry with me," he said, "because we didn't discuss the decision with you first."

These clients had such confidence in me that one was actually mad at the other one for not consulting with me! This story illustrates the level of confidence you should inspire in your clients. Confidence is an essential quality for every entrepreneur and leader. The more confident you are in yourself, and the more you are able to project that confidence, the more faith your clients will have in you. You want your clients to have so much confidence in you that they feel they *must* get your advice before making a big decision.

CONFIDENCE FLOWS FROM KNOWLEDGE OF YOUR SUBJECT MATTER

So how do you start? How do you acquire the self-confidence that will then make your clients confident in you? The most important step is the easiest to explain, but the hardest to do: you must have true subject matter mastery. We all understand that true expertise is critical, but many entrepreneurs actually fall short. Some think they don't have time for continuing education and professional development or feel that what they already know is good enough. It's not. To be successful in the face of your competition, you can never stop seeking out new knowledge and improving your practice.

The world changes every day. We must always be learning in order to keep up and make the most of our opportunities. Running a business is like running a race: if you stop learning, your confidence will falter, and you will fall behind. If your training is lacking, then fear and avoidance will creep in. The same is true in any line of work. Lack of confidence is often a symptom of insufficient knowledge and subject matter mastery. To stay ahead in the race, you need to constantly become more of an expert. Continually updating your knowledge will increase your confidence, which in turn will grow your business. If you learn as much as possible about your field and never stop learning, then you can be fearless.

PRACTICAL STRATEGIES FOR MAKING TIME TO IMPROVE

Most professional licenses require a certain number of

continuing education hours per year in order to keep the license current. I take several courses a year in order to stay up-to-date with the ever-changing laws and regulations impacting my work. Many professionals do the minimum number of hours required to stay licensed, and they consider that to be a sufficient investment of time. Again, it's not. The licensing requirements are a good launching point for staying current, but if you want to stand out, take as many courses as you have time for, not just the minimum required. Courses take place online or in person, so there are many opportunities available. Attend in-person seminars and talk to people about your work while you're there. Read everything you can on your subject. Keep up with the latest technology. Continual self-improvement allows us to rise to the top.

But how do you make the time? The American business community is exceptional, in part, because we work so hard. Oftentimes, though, we get so busy with the immediate, day-to-day concerns of our business that our continuing education falls behind. One way to make time for expanding our knowledge base is an increased focus on delegation. Reevaluate your business process to determine if more activities can be delegated to employees. If you try to do everything by yourself, you'll struggle to keep up. I'm always looking for elements of my business that I can delegate to my employees so that I can attend important continuing education conferences. Delegation allows me to invest time in growing my subject matter expertise and allows my employees to grow their careers by learning new responsibilities.

If you have a seed stage or early stage company and don't have a large team to delegate to, you can still block out time on a regular basis to concentrate on building knowledge. For example, once a week, try blocking off the morning. During one session, you can read articles on an emerging aspect of your field. During another, you can go through modules of a continuing education course. Later, you can go through client portfolios in depth to look for underlying issues and patterns. When I block out time in my schedule, I don't take calls. My receptionist takes messages for me—she knows how important communication is for us, so I still receive urgent messages, but otherwise I respond later in the day. It takes discipline to block out regular sessions in your schedule for continuing education, and that discipline pays dividends over time. Make learning a part of your routine.

Some may think that taking extra continuing education courses or blocking off time on a regular basis to focus on professional development sound like great ideas in theory but are impossible to execute in practice. Ultimately, making the time comes down to motivation. I feel motivated to devote this time to learning because I know my efforts serve my goal of being a leading expert in my field. When a client asks me a question about a specific investment product, will I know what to say? My answer has to be yes, because if I fumble, the client will lose confidence in me and take their business elsewhere.

Take a moment to close your eyes and ask yourself how your level of expertise truly compares with your competition. Are you at the forefront of knowledge in your field? Are you average? Are there areas where you're falling behind? Have you done everything you can to learn about each relevant subject in sufficient depth? Listen for the honest answer within yourself. If you feel you're not quite where you want to be, dedicate yourself to making the time to learn. Remember, with true subject matter mastery, you can be fearless and confident. And when you are confident, you generate and retain business. It's that simple.

DISPLAYING YOUR KNOWLEDGE

Once you have mastery of your area, you'll be excited to share your knowledge. You'll want people to ask you questions. And if your clients ask you a question you don't have a good answer to, be honest. Tell them you need to do more research and will get back to them. Then, make sure to do the research and follow up promptly. If you're constantly striving to know everything you can about your work, then you'll have the confidence to be transparent when you need to do some more research before responding to a question. And next time you get that question, you'll know the answer.

Deep knowledge of your field will also make you more confident presenting or speaking publicly on your area of expertise. If your knowledge is shaky, your presentation will be shaky. But if your knowledge is sound, you will be confident and make a good impression. Being a subject matter expert allows you to take advantage of these opportunities to showcase your knowledge. For example, I often go on radio programs to answer questions live. The shows are an extreme test of my confidence. Once I'm on though, I'm not preoccupied with making a mistake. I'm not nervous or hesitant, because I have confidence in my knowledge base. And you'll be just as confident when you know your subject. Knowledge is your power.

PROVIDING COMPLETE INFORMATION TO CLIENTS

On the other hand, not becoming an expert in your field can lead to negative business practices. For example, some business owners use the short-sighted strategy of withholding information from their customers, thinking that this practice will make those customers dependent and force them to keep returning for more help. This type of business practice is the result of a lack of confidence in what you are offering to your customers and can ultimately stop your business from achieving growth.

I see this practice in the tax accounting world. For instance, some accountants give their clients copies of the completed tax forms but not the underlying worksheets. These accountants worry that if they hand over all the information used to prepare the forms, the clients could simply take that information to a different tax preparer the following year or use it to prepare the documents themselves.

My approach is completely the opposite. I give copies of all the underlying worksheets to my clients. If for some reason I wasn't able to prepare their taxes next year, I would want them to have the information they needed to make a smooth transition to a different tax preparer. I don't want to set up unnecessary hurdles by depriving them of details and documents related to their own taxes. My goal is not to give clients the minimum amount of information so that they feel dependent on me; my focus is on providing transparent, exemplary service.

If you're knowledgeable and confident, you will feel comfortable being fully transparent with your clients as well. By the time I'm done sharing my knowledge with them, they see why I'm offering particular solutions and what the next steps should be. I'm teaching them relevant concepts, deepening their understanding, and improving their ability to make good decisions. As a result, they want to work with me. I even tell my clients if they want to take the information I've given them and use it to find products or services elsewhere, that's okay—I'm just glad they're making an informed decision. How often do I go through such a detailed, tailored explanation only to have a client take their business elsewhere? Very rarely.

Over the long term, if you are confident that you're striving to offer the best service you can, then there is no reason to withhold information from your clients. In fact, by being open, honest and transparent, you will gain your clients' trust and loyalty to your brand. If you're the best in your field, people will seek you out rather than trying to get what they can from you and moving on to someone else. If your clients are confident that you are looking out for them and serving them with integrity, they will be grateful and want to stick with you.

CONFIDENCE MAKES AN IMPRESSION

When clients first approach me, they often ask how much I charge. I tell them the services will cost a fair fee. I feel confident in the value of the service that I will provide, and I want to earn their fee. But if I haven't earned it, they shouldn't have to pay. So when I meet clients for the first time, I tell them that by the time they leave my office, three thoughts should go through their minds or I'll give them a refund.

First, I want them to think that I'm knowledgeable in my subject area and that I'm providing them with relevant, fact-based, valuable information. Second, I want them to wonder why they didn't come to see me sooner. And third, I want them to be glad they've finally come to see me now. If I make those three impressions on them, I've earned my fee.

It's common for new clients to call me as soon as they get home or even return from the office parking lot to tell me that those three thoughts are in fact running through their mind. That's the value of knowledge and confidence. They tell me that not only are they leaving with those three impressions, but they benefitted from our session so much that they feel compelled to refer a relative or a friend. That kind of feedback gives me even more confidence.

CONFIDENCE REMOVES DOUBTS

I have clients of all ages, but I particularly enjoy working with younger clients who are just starting out in life. Many years ago, a young advertising salesman named Larry visited my office. He felt uncertain about his financial future. I worked with him on specific strategies for his financial well-being, but I also gave him a piece of general advice: no matter how much or how little you make, set aside some to invest so you benefit from compounding returns over time. Since he was just starting to earn an income, Larry had his doubts about saving, but he was confident in me and followed the advice. Larry eventually moved across the country, but we always remained in touch. When my business had a celebration to commemorate its twenty-fifth anniversary, Larry attended and spoke on stage. He talked about some of the doubts he had as a younger man and how we wind up regretting many of the decisions we make in our youth. But working with me as his financial advisor was one decision he will never regret. He said I eased his doubts, and he couldn't have achieved financial success without my help.

When I'm confident, I can remove doubts and insecurities in others and give them their own confidence. If a client comes to me feeling nervous or with doubts, I know I can alleviate any concerns. It is an extremely rewarding experience that leaves me joyful and grateful.

The rewards of passing on what you've acquired bring us to our final "C"—Contribute.

KEY LESSONS

- Knowledge is the key source of confidence. As an entrepreneur, it's essential for you to make time to learn everything you can about your field. Lack of knowledge leads to insecurity, poor business practices and losing clients. When you are a true expert, your clients will see that confidence and feel that they must consult with you.

- Find ways to showcase your knowledge. Being knowledgeable will give you the confidence to answer your clients' questions as well as to tell them when you don't know an answer. Don't be afraid to be honest when you don't have an answer at your fingertips. It's easier to say, "I don't know, let me get back to you," when you already know a lot.

- Clients and customers must feel confident that they're in good hands. Your own confidence will make your clients leave thinking, "Wow, he knows what he's talking about! Why didn't we come see him before? Well, at least we've come to him now!"

CHAPTER SIX

CONTRIBUTE:
MAKE A VISIBLE DIFFERENCE

"I shall pass through this world but once. Any good therefore that I can do or any kindness that I can show to any human being, let me do it now. Let me not defer or neglect it, for I shall not pass this way again."

—STEPHEN GRELLET,
FRENCH-AMERICAN MISSIONARY

As a result of the path my life has taken, I feel an obligation to use my business to contribute and help improve the lives of others. We started our journey through The 5 C's by highlighting that entrepreneurs have a duty to give back. Entrepreneurs and the communities that they work in are extremely codependent. Businesses succeed or fail based on the community's interest and support. Similarly, communities rise or fall based on the contributions of its entrepreneurs. None of us achieves success alone, and I don't think we should be enjoying the benefits of that success alone either.

True philanthropy involves contributing because you're inspired by a cause, not because you're seeking a reward. Find ways to make contributions that align with the values and mission of your company without trying to use the contribution to advertise your business. By promoting your values instead of promoting your company, you will make the most fulfilling impact. Let the rest work itself out. The return on investment will be the positive effect you have on the lives of others.

That being said, it is still important to publicize your contributions—not for the purpose of promoting yourself or your business, but for the purpose of inspiring others. If you engage in philanthropy, the community should be aware of it. Visible contributions encourage others to join in and contribute as well. A story in the news about how a business owner used his company to contribute to the community may inspire other business owners to do the same. Publicity around giving can create a ripple effect of generosity. In this chapter, I'll share some examples of the contributions I've made—not to seek praise for those contributions, but to hopefully inspire you, as a fellow entrepreneur, to use your business to make a contribution in any way you can.

CONTRIBUTING YOUR SERVICES

All successful businesses have an important product or service to offer. You might consider ways to contribute these products or services to positively impact the community. For example, my business provides free tax preparation services to veterans and firefighters. These people have made the ultimate sacrifice for their community; they go to work not knowing if they'll come home that night. Veterans have risked their lives protecting our country, and firefighters have died in the line of duty in my city. Helping them free of charge is a way for me to show my gratitude.

One of my clients, an Air Force veteran named Gary Boucher, once gave me the ultimate present. He had earned a medal of good conduct during his service and gave it to me, framed with a personal note of thanks for the contributions I've made to veterans and the community at large. He said he didn't know how much longer he would be alive, but he wanted me to have the medal because of the respect I show to veterans. I was very touched, but I felt he should keep the medal in his family. I called him, thanked him, and told him I was honored— but it was his medal and he should keep it. However, he insisted, saying his son felt the same way. He told me he wanted me to keep the medal because he thought if anyone deserved a good conduct award in our community, it should be me. The medal is still proudly displayed in my office.

Air Force Veteran Gary Boucher's Personal Medal of Good Conduct

THE PIANO

Aside from contributing your products and services, entrepreneurs can look for ways to make additional visible contributions that will inspire others to get involved. Reaching out to your city government, planning board or other community organization can be a great way to find these types of opportunities. Communities often need help with various projects, from building a bridge, to improving a park, to installing benches. Possibilities abound for you to give back as an entrepreneur.

One morning, I read a notice in the paper from the Worcester Senior Center, a community center focused on improving the lives of senior citizens. The notice said that for many years someone would come play the senior center's piano for the elderly residents. The residents enjoyed it very much. Unfortunately, though, the piano was no longer playable. The center wanted to know if someone in the community might have an old one to donate.

Reading this story immediately gave me the urge to help.

After talking to my wife, I called the senior center and asked them for more details on the type of piano they were looking for. I explained that I was a local business owner looking to help out in the community. I said that if it was within my budget, I would like to buy them a new instrument. They were amazed that I would be willing to buy them something new and were thrilled at the prospect.

I then spoke with the owner of a local piano shop who was able to find an instrument meeting both my company's budget and the center's specifications. I purchased and donated the piano to the center. The shop owner, who was a great pianist in his own right, came to play at an event inaugurating the new instrument. Even the mayor and city councilors attended.

I dedicated the piano to my Guru and the commitment to service he inspired in me. My company made this donation because we wanted to help, not because we expected anything in return. Many of the senior citizens approached us and said they hoped God blessed us for our generosity. Those blessings were reward enough; we weren't trying to drum up new tax clients. As it turned out, there was an article about the event in the local newspaper, so the word got out that our business cared about contributing to the community.

THE LITTLE LEAGUE FIELD

My older son grew up playing baseball. Games were typically held at the local Little League field. One year, as part of a statewide tournament, his team played on another field—a lighted field where games could be played at night. The kids felt like they were at Fenway Park! They were glowing with happiness and excitement to be under the lights like professional ball players. Seeing their joy, I told my wife that I hoped we could purchase lights for our local Little League field one day, so future generations of kids could feel the same sense of excitement on their home turf. Our children will inherit our community, and if I can make a contribution to inspire them and sow the seeds of giving back, I will.

Many years later, as my business continued to grow, we approached the league to discuss the possibility of lighting the field. We got approval from the city and contributed state-of-the-art lights for the field. For the inauguration, my sons were invited to come back from college and throw out the first pitch under the new lights. Today, because of the lights, the Little League State Championship games are being played on that field. For me, the reward of donating is not business development; it's seeing the enjoyment of the kids who play under the lights. They feel like professional ball players, just as my son's team did the first time they saw such lights.

Our local league also installed a bench with an engraved plaque noting that the lights were donated by the Mitras, owners of The Guru Tax and Financial Services. One day, my grandchildren can play there and feel proud of their family's contributions to the community. We might be gone by then, but we will have passed on our values. I hope my actions will inspire them to be similarly generous when they grow up.

Lights at Joe Schwartz Little League Field in Worcester, MA
and plaque honoring our contribution

CONTRIBUTIONS FROM MY WIFE

A group of students once asked Warren Buffet for the secret of his success. Buffet said the secret is having a partner who understands his philosophy of life and always supports him. I completely agree with him.

My wife and I have known each other since childhood.

In 1980, I returned to India so we could get married and I could bring her to America with me. When our first son was born, raising him became her focus. Because I grew up without a mother, I wanted to ensure our children would have a loving, consistent relationship with their mother. My wife is educated and had a job, but she quit in order to devote herself to raising our son. Then, when our second son was born, she decided to start a daycare center out of our home. This way, she was able to be there for our children while still having a job and bringing in an income.

She has always helped and inspired me to fulfill my goals and pursue my purpose. We have been through many struggles together. When I changed careers and we had very little money, she did everything she could to make the transition possible. She was home with our two sons, who were six and three years old at the time, and she still did whatever it took to support the business. There were times when she worked two jobs to try to supplement our income.

My wife has put a tremendous amount of energy into mothering our sons. She made many sacrifices, including professional ones. She has valued and supported my philosophy about the importance of a mother's love. As an intelligent, educated woman, she had to swallow her pride in the early years when people didn't understand her decision. Our boys have benefited so much from growing up on her lap, with the consistency of her love.

In return, I always prioritize my wife. If she needs me to be there, I'm there. We have become so close that we don't know how we'd live without each other. Our relationship is based on deep understanding. I may be the one receiving praise from clients for how we run our business or from community leaders for our contributions to the community, while she remains an unsung heroine. When I come home, though, I tell her about the successes and let her know that it's all because of her.

For our twenty-fifth wedding anniversary, we planted a cherry tree that we call "The Motherhood Tree," since a huge theme and priority of our relationship has been motherhood. When our boys were very young, there was a time when Sheema was very ill, and we weren't sure if she was going to make it. I prayed to God she would recover so my two sons would experience what I could not—growing up with a mother. And, fortunately, my prayers were answered. Now, every year, this tree blooms on Mother's Day, true to its name—and I'm so grateful she's still here as my wife and mother to our sons. Having a close-knit, loving family has given me the strength to succeed in business, and my success has, in turn, contributed to the well-being of my family. The two go hand-in-hand.

STARTING OUR FOUNDATION

Many of the contributions my wife and I make to the community today were inspired by a horrible incident.

In 2015, my wife and I were in Brazil for a Rotary International convention. My hip was bothering me at the time, so I was walking with a cane. But it was a beautiful evening with a full moon, so we decided to go for a walk along Copacabana Beach in Rio. As it was a popular tourist area, we didn't think it could be dangerous. We were wrong.

As it turned out, my wife was badly attacked by two muggers. She started screaming, "Help! Help!" and tried to stop them from taking her jewelry and belongings. I attempted to intervene, and I broke my cane into three pieces hitting the attackers with it. They threw me to the ground—it was like a violent movie. They got away with my wife's cell phone, and she had bruises on her face, but we were fortunate not to be seriously injured. Many people have been stabbed or killed for resisting these muggings in Brazil. The police said they were surprised we survived. We still have nightmares about it.

When we returned home, it took some time to heal, both physically and emotionally. We felt lucky to have made it through together, but we wanted something good to come out of the incident. After much thought and discussion about how to turn the experience into something positive, we started a program offering free self-defense classes for women. The goal is to give women the confidence to handle situations like the one Sheema experienced in Brazil. Through the program, we have trained almost 400 women and girls in self-defense. Sheema has also been invited to speak about the work at a city women's conference.

After we began sponsoring the free lessons, we wanted to expand our charitable work and our mission of helping the community. We founded Joy Guru Humanitarian Services. I always remember the moment when I went to visit my Guru in a temple in India and asked for his blessing to use his name in the tax practice. He had agreed, so long as I used the business as a vehicle to help the community. Now, we give excess proceeds from our business or my speaking engagements to the foundation, which is also named in his honor.

The foundation's slogan is "Helping and restoring hope for those who feel helpless and hopeless." In addition to the self-defense classes, the foundation also supports many humanitarian causes that are close to my heart. For instance, I was homeless as a child, so now we offer a monthly lunch to the homeless. I feel so grateful to have gone from being without a home to having enough financial success that I can play a small part in helping others in the same situation.

We also help people who are visually impaired. I mentioned earlier that my father went blind when I was young. He could not be cured because we did not have the money for him to see a specialist. His condition was curable, but he died blind because of financial reasons. Now, the foundation works to prevent this situation from befalling others.

One of the key goals of the foundation, which has now been recognized as an IRS 501(c)(3) charitable organization, continues to be making visible contributions to inspire others to contribute as well. For instance, the foundation established a scholarship that will help pay the tuition for a financially challenged high school graduate who would like to attend Worcester State University for higher education. Additionally, the foundation sponsored Oved Rico, a high school student, who had the talent and desire to join the Worcester Youth Orchestra, but not the funds. Oved's parents were both immigrants who worked multiple jobs, and Oved himself worked a part-time job in order to support his parents and his siblings, whom he also cared for. Despite his challenges, Oved was passionate about music and wanted to pursue playing the French horn. Joy Guru Humanitarian Services provided financial aid for Oved so he could join the orchestra, and we will continue to support him along the way. Recently, Oved was selected by the Commonwealth of Massachusetts to be part of a group of musicians who will give a presentation in Washington D.C. We are proud of giving Oved the opportunity to fulfill his dream and passion.

Thanks to fundraising and the generosity of the community, we are also working on financing the construction of a humanitarian center to be named Joy Guru International Humanitarian Center. The humanitarian center will have a free eye clinic, a winter homeless shelter that provides meals, and a school that will offer self-defense lessons and classes to children on good citizenship, personal finance, public speaking, and leadership. I envision the center including a library and an auditorium for motivational speakers to come and inspire the community. The humanitarian center itself will stand as a tangible reminder to people to get involved and give back.

I believe at the end of the day, if someone asks you whether you've touched another life, you should be able to answer with a resounding "yes." We're tremendously fortunate as entrepreneurs to be able to help others in need. Bill Gates has done a huge amount of philanthropic work through his foundation, but your company doesn't have to be as large as his to contribute. Small business owners can also give back to their communities, share what they've done, and inspire others to do the same. Connect with your community and contribute.

KEY LESSONS

- The ultimate achievement as an entrepreneur lies in what you contribute. Giving back is the real essence of success.

- Though giving should be motivated by your values and not in expectation of a reward, contributing to the community does build a positive reputation for your business. People will see you not only as a business owner but also as a person who cares. By publicizing your actions, you can help inspire generosity in others.

- Using your business to make a contribution is personally rewarding in an emotional and spiritual sense. You will know that your business made the community a better place.

CHAPTER SEVEN

LEADERSHIP:
GUIDE YOUR COMMUNITY ORGANIZATION

"The greatest leader is not necessarily the one who does the greatest things. He is the one that gets the people to do the greatest things."

—RONALD REAGAN,
40TH PRESIDENT OF THE UNITED STATES

The 5 C's are not just a tool for successfully running a business. The same 5 C's can also guide you to becoming an effective leader of a community organization, whether or not you are an entrepreneur. Truly anyone can apply The 5 C's to rise to the challenge of leading organizations in the community.

BECOMING A LEADER

The first step in becoming a great leader is actually believing you can be a great leader. So, each day when you have a quiet moment, consider your dreams and give yourself encouragement that you can achieve them. Positive self-talk cultivates optimism and helps focus on your goals. Every day, I look in the mirror and tell myself, "You can do it." As you seize the opportunities that will carry you in the right direction, and as you continue to encourage yourself, you'll develop the qualities of a leader.

I always remember the story of a young boy who dreaded going to school because the school had a physical education requirement. This boy didn't like to get sweaty or exert himself. He really did not want to play a sport. Begrudgingly, he finally decided to sign up for tennis. He figured he could stand on one side of a net, hit the ball back, not get shoved or too sweaty, and meet the school requirement.

When school started, he was in last place on the tennis team. But to his surprise, he found tennis interesting and fun. He felt motivated to show up on time, practice, and make an effort to play better. The boy told his father what he'd really like to do was become captain of the team. He knew he was the worst player, though, so he didn't think he would have a shot.

His father told him being captain isn't just about how

well you play—it's also about having leadership abilities. A captain leads the team by motivating and supporting the other players. His father advised him to take an interest in his teammates. If they fell down, he should help them up and make sure they were okay. If someone broke a racket, he could offer to lend his in its place. He might not be the best *player* on the team, but he could be the best *supporter* of the team, cheering on his teammates to feel good about themselves and play at their highest level.

His father also told him to speak positively to himself. Every day, he should focus on his desire to become captain, reassure himself he could do so, and then pay attention to the opportunities that arose to get him closer to his goal. The boy kept working toward his goal, and the more effort he put into being a great member of the team, the better he played. He started winning more games, and he improved his ranking.

At the end of the season, there was an awards ceremony. The boy came home from school that day with his jacket wrapped around something, and he asked his parents to look at what was inside: it was a plaque, on which the boy's name was engraved alongside the word "Captain."

As you might have guessed, the boy was my youngest son. Knowing how much he wanted to be captain and how hard he worked to achieve that role, I teared up when I saw the plaque. My wife and I asked him how he did it. He said he told himself every day, "I want to be captain. I want to be captain." Then, he put in the work to achieve his dream.

THE BEST QUALITIES IN A LEADER

My father encouraged me to be a good, honest, and ethical leader. He taught me such leaders have four qualities.

First, good leaders are genuinely concerned about the people around them—teammates, employees, clients, or others. Second, they're willing to sacrifice for the greater good in order to benefit their team. Third, they always have a goal in mind; they know what they're trying to achieve and why, and they have a plan to get there. Fourth, when they walk toward that goal, they make sure everyone walks with them. A leader's primary job is to inspire.

I apply my father's principles to any leadership position in my life, whether I'm making decisions for my business or leading a community organization. I've also found that taking ownership and being enthusiastic are essential. Any time I am given an opportunity to lead an organization, I treat the organization the same way as I would my own business. When I am enthusiastic about the cause, and treat the organization as my own, I wake up every day looking forward to the work I'm going to do to steer the organization in the right direction. If you cultivate the practice of enthusiastically thinking every day about the organization you lead, solutions start to present themselves. You feel inspired, and you inspire the people around you.

The best leaders are those who challenge themselves every day—the people who dream big. Dreams are the precursors to reality. John F. Kennedy dreamed of landing a man on the moon, and America did that. Gandhi dreamed of bringing freedom to India without violence, and he and his followers did so. Nelson Mandela never gave up on his dream of ending apartheid, even while imprisoned for twenty-seven years, and he became the president of South Africa. Every good leader has to dream and set their sights high. My dream for my foundation, Joy Guru Humanitarian Services, is that it will have a worldwide reputation for ensuring every dollar donated goes directly to helping humanitarian causes and bringing balance to the world. If you have a dream in mind from the very beginning, you can start taking steps toward making it come true.

USING THE 5 C'S TO LEAD A COMMUNITY ORGANIZATION

If your dream is to lead a community organization, you can get there with positive thinking and hard work. But the most daunting task comes after you have risen to a position of leadership. How do you effectively lead the organization? The same 5 C's—Connect, Communicate, Create, Confidence, and Contribute—will provide a firm foundation for successfully leading your organization.

I have had the honor of leading several community organizations. Whether as a president, board member, or committee chairperson, my approach has always been to make a positive impact and advance the mission of the organizations I lead. To do that, I use The 5 C's. For me, The 5 C's are more than theoretical concepts—they are the framework that guides my decisions and actions.

I would like to share my experience with the Worcester Rotary Club to help demonstrate how The 5 C's can help you successfully lead a community organization. I joined Rotary in 2008, in part, because I was strongly drawn to the Rotary's motto, "Service above self." The motto emphasizes thinking beyond your own worries and focusing on contributing to others. Five years after I joined, our club made me the president. Here's how I used The 5 C's to leave an impact on the organization.

CONNECT

The more you connect with people, both inside and outside your organization, the more you can achieve as the leader of that organization. It's your responsibility to take the initiative. If there was a Rotary Club breakfast or lunch meeting, rather than spending the time eating, I would often go around, say hi, shake everyone's hand, and see how they're doing. Many conversations I had were more personal and not really about the organization. For example, if I talked to someone at the meeting who was having car trouble, I would gladly offer to give him or her a ride. There are dozens of opportunities, large and small, to forge connections with people and help them see that you genuinely care about them. Winning people's hearts is key to achieving great things.

Through connecting with the club members, I also learned their thoughts on the organization. I was able to appreciate that many members felt that energy was lacking within the club and they were dismayed by dwindling membership numbers. At one time, the club had 350 members, but when I took over, enrollment was down to 48. Leaders need to understand the deficits of the current situation so they can determine how to address those deficits and lift up the people within an organization—connecting with and understanding those people is a key first step.

In addition to forming connections within the organization, the more you connect with leaders of other organizations, the more you can leverage your potential as a leader. Cross-connections among organizations are important. You can work together to elevate everyone's mission and achieve your collective goals. When I was President of the Rotary Club, we created partnerships with the Boys & Girls Club of Worcester and the Worcester Community Action Council, and we all benefited because of the connections between the organizations' leaders.

COMMUNICATE

Strong communication is key to successful leadership, just as poor communication is often the reason behind a failure of leadership. Communicating face-to-face is one of the most effective tools at your disposal. During my induction as President of the Rotary Club, I clearly communicated my goals for the year. Specifically, I told everyone that I wanted to add fifty new members by the end of my term. That number is unheard of in the Rotary world. If you can add five new members in a year, it is considered a success. But I felt we could achieve my goal. I continued to communicate this message to all the members at every meeting. My slogan was "member per member"—each member should strive to bring in one additional member. I told them to go talk to the people they knew, personally and professionally—their doctors, lawyers, accountants, plumbers, hair stylists, and so on. Just bring in one new person to a meeting so we could meet face-to-face and persuade that person to join.

Communicating outside of your organization is just as important. You must make your organization's mission and efforts to achieve that mission known to the public. Using local television and radio is an effective way to leverage the power of communication. If you approach a local station and say you'd like to spend five minutes talking about how your organization helps the community, most will give you the time. I've been on multiple radio shows to talk about various organizations, including the Rotary Club. I emphasize how we help the community and how others can get engaged with our mission to help as well. When you share with people how you're giving back, they recognize your genuineness. Your positive communication inspires them to join your cause.

CREATE

For a leader of a community organization, creativity involves figuring out innovative ways to make people aware of the exceptional work your organization does. Whatever you do, you should be different, authentic, and not afraid to take some risks. Every organization is different, but you can find unique ways to make your organization stand out.

For example, I had noticed that many of the billboards

and posters in my city had been replaced by digital signage—LED boards controlled by computer software. So I saw which local businesses were advertising on the digital boards, and I approached the business owners with a simple request: would they consider adding a short message at the bottom of their digital sign? "Join Rotary—Make a Difference" or "Join Rotary—Help the Community." Making a change to those digital signs is relatively easy—just a few keystrokes on a computer. Many business owners were willing to do so to help our organization. Their businesses also benefited from the positive association with a respected community organization. Since we got creative, we received free publicity, boosted awareness of our organization and increased our membership.

Your organization will no doubt be different and you'll come up with your own creative ideas that work in your case. But the key is to continue to think creatively. Do not be afraid to try a new approach. The creative process will help inspire solutions, set your organization apart, and make you an effective leader.

CONFIDENCE

Just as knowledge of your subject matter is crucial for having confidence as an entrepreneur, knowledge of your organization is crucial for becoming a confident leader.

The more you know, the more confident you become. What is the history of the organization? Who founded it? What are the new initiatives? How many employees are there? What is the budget? What is the revenue stream? Each group has a different mission, set of activities, and history. When you immerse yourself in the specifics, you can speak to community members and leaders knowledgeably about your organization. In turn, they will have faith that the work is worthwhile and in good hands. To lead an organization confidently, you must first know each and every thing about it.

No matter which organization I am leading, I take the time to learn the details and mission of that organization inside and out. Having that detailed knowledge at my fingertips provides me with the confidence to represent the group in public and answer any question that might come up. As soon as I became President of the Rotary Club, I set about learning as much as I could about Rotary in general and our club in particular. I wanted to know about its history, mission, vision, achievements—everything. For example, the organization has helped eradicate polio from all but two countries in the world, directly vaccinating children by hand. The group also helps provide clean water and scholarships to the underprivileged. With this knowledge, I can confidently approach anyone to talk about the organization. Who wouldn't want to be a part of our club? Who wouldn't want to get involved to help with such causes? Knowledge leads to confidence, and you can be sure that this confidence will be felt by anyone you speak with about your organization.

CONTRIBUTE

As a leader of a community organization, you are already contributing. But simply being a decision-maker and manager of the organization is not enough contribution to make you an effective leader. To be a successful leader of an organization, you must continue to be an active member of that organization as well. Even though you are the leader and are setting the goals, you must continue to contribute toward achieving those goals alongside the other members.

As Rotary Club President, I had set the bold goal of growing our club by 50 members, a number well above any past membership increase. At the end of my term, we had 82 new members! Membership grew from 48 to 130 over the course of a single year, greatly exceeding my goal. The membership drive was successful, in part, because I didn't just set the goal; I contributed toward achieving it. I brought in 55 new members during this period.

But honestly, I'm most proud of the 27 brought in by other members. Those 27 represent the fact that other members were motivated by my contribution and decided to contribute themselves. I had inspired my team to expand our mission and touch more lives. The following year, I was honored by the President of Rotary International, because bringing in 82 new members in a single term is a world record for the organization.

Because of such unprecedented success, that year, the District voted our club to be the Best Rotary Club of the Year for the first time in the 103 years of the club's existence. Since then, I've had the opportunity to speak at Rotary events all over the world to teach and inspire people to replicate what I did and bring new life to their local Rotary clubs and districts. The President of Rotary International made me an advisor of the organization's membership committee. And for Rotary International's centennial year, under my leadership, we were able to raise $1.3 million in only nine months—an amount that normally takes two to three years to bring in.

With these successes, I've been honored as Rotarian of the Year twice. The mayor has given the key to the city both to the Rotary Club of Worcester and to me personally for outstanding community service. And recently, my wife and I were given an honor by Worcester State University for our community service.

The recognition is an honor and is humbling. It brings tears to my eyes that I can give back to the people around me and that they feel moved to thank me in meaningful ways. It reinforces to me the value of authentic leadership and the opportunity to make a difference—anyone can do it with the right framework, attitude and work ethic. I used The 5 C's to make these achievements possible, and you can apply the same model to any situation. I connected with my team, communicated our goals, creatively spread our message, inspired the community with my confidence as a leader, and contributed to the effort right alongside the rest of the members. So can you.

KEY LESSONS

- Believe that you can be a leader of a community organization. Every day, tell yourself, "I can do it!" Inspire yourself first to put yourself in a position to inspire others.

- Use The 5 C's as a framework to achieve success as a leader of a community organization and remember the qualities of a good leader. Win the hearts of your team by being concerned about them, sacrificing for them, setting a firm goal and walking with them to achieve that goal.

- Have big dreams for your organization. Your members will follow you if you take ownership of those dreams and contribute alongside everyone else.

CONCLUSION

My life story has had its ups and downs. I've felt pain and seen suffering, but I've also felt healing and seen compassion. These experiences guided me to where I am today. When I think about where I started and look at where I am now, I can't help but feel a tremendous sense of gratitude. So many people contributed to my success. My father, who left me his wisdom. My brother and sister-in-law, who carried me through my education. The travel agent, who showed me true selflessness. My Guru, who helped guide the course of my career and the mission of my business. My wife, who sacrificed and has provided unyielding support. And many, many others.

Thanks to these people and these life experiences, I was in a position to develop The 5 C's—Connect, Communicate, Create, Confidence, and Contribute. The 5 C's were the key to success as both an entrepreneur and a community leader. My life experiences and the countless people who guided me along the way made me want to pay my success and good fortune forward if I ever got the chance. The true essence of success, as I've said many times, is to be able to give back and touch another life. If we can achieve success through entrepreneurship and then give back, we complete the cycle of living fully and helping the next generation to do so as well. Applying The 5 C's gives us a roadmap for impacting other lives and feeling satisfied at the end of ours.

I WANT YOU TO BE PROUD OF ME

I often wear a pin that says, "I Want You to be Proud of Me." I've given the same pin to my family and employees. I wear the pin because I want my employees to feel proud to work for me, and I want my community to be proud of the work I do through the various organizations I am involved in.

We will all face a day when we will tell the next generation what we've accomplished. At that time, we'll either be proud of what we've done or feel ashamed. You don't want to be one of the people who is ashamed. You have the opportunity to take the next step toward true success by giving back as an entrepreneur and a leader. Take that opportunity and make the next generation proud of you.

I always believe that whatever I do, my acts and engagements should serve as an example for others, starting with my sons. I want them to see the reasons behind what I do and then be the next to carry the torch. My grandchildren can then continue the mission. Together, we can light the candle of inspiration in others and bring brightness to our community. I hope through this book I will add more lights to the world—even one more would be a success.

TURNING NEGATIVES INTO POSITIVES

My sister got married when she was fourteen years old. Weddings are huge celebrations in India. People typically make the events as lavish as possible, but my family was poor, so we didn't have the means for my sister's wedding to be fancy.

I was only four years old at the time, and my mother was no longer with us, so my sister tried to take care of me as best as she could. The night before the wedding, she brought me one of my shirts—the least worn-out one she could find—and told me to put it under my pillow. We didn't have an iron, so she said that by placing the shirt under my pillow and sleeping on it, the shirt would look like it had been ironed. She was doing what she could with what little we had to make a good impression for the wedding celebration.

I still marvel at how much my situation has changed since then. I've benefitted from many opportunities to improve my life and can now share with others. I've been given a tremendous gift in having a successful business, and I want to complete the story by helping to lift others up in my community.

I recently read an article written by the superintendent of Worcester's public schools detailing the issues faced by students living in poverty. Many don't have the resources to purchase new clothes. And they don't even have access to a washer and dryer, so what they wear is dirty. The superintendent asked if anyone in the community would be willing to donate some new shirts. I reached out to her, and she told me there are three schools in particular where a high percentage of the students live in poverty. So for these three schools, Joy Guru Humanitarian Services bought over 1,000 uniform shirts with the school logo on them for the students.

Donating uniforms to Worcester Public School students

It is immensely gratifying to have gone from having one worn-out shirt that could only be "ironed" by placing it under my pillow to being able to give more than 1,000 students brand-new shirts. I'm filled with joy and pride by seeing the happiness and gratitude on the faces of the students who can now wear nice, clean clothes.

We all go through negative experiences in our lives. We can shut ourselves off and say, "Why me?" Or, we can turn those negative experiences into something positive. Many of the challenges I have faced throughout life have shaped how I contribute to my community. In my foundation, there is a reason behind everything we do. We turn negatives into positives. I was homeless as a child; now, I help the homeless. My father died blind; now, I help the blind and visually impaired. My wife was attacked in Brazil; now, I help fund self-defense classes for women and girls. I dream of the day when the Joy Guru International Humanitarian Center will be built so that we can provide more services to women, children, the blind, and the homeless at the humanitarian center. Through the humanitarian center, we will continue to take any negatives that come in and send them back out as positive hope for society.

You too can transform your negative experiences and have a positive impact. Find the causes that resonate with you. Every day, we read about tragedies, scandals, and problems in the news. Who else will solve the world's many problems if not us? We must step up and help address the issues we want to change. The important thing is recognizing you have a responsibility to the world, identifying worthwhile causes you care about, and then getting involved.

DELIVER YOUR PACKAGES

When babies are born, they have both of their fists clenched. I believe we're born on this Earth holding two packages sent by our creator—one in each clenched fist. In one fist, we hold our responsibility to ourselves, our family, and our children. We must give them the best life possible. In the other fist, we hold our responsibility to others. That responsibility could be to an individual person, it could be to your community, it could be to your city or country, or even the whole world.

When we die, our palms lie open. Either we've forgotten, lost, or thrown away our two packages—or we've delivered them. I suggest we all deliver what we were born holding in our fists. The real success story is not the size of our bank balance, the house we own, the car we drive, or the suit we wear. The essential questions at the end of the day are: Have I made a difference? Have I touched another life? Have I given someone else hope? Have I delivered both packages I was born with? The answers to those questions are the essence of success in entrepreneurship, in leadership and in life.

When I'm old, I want to have wonderful, inspiring stories to tell my grandchildren. I want to tell them the conditions I lived through and what I did to improve situations facing others. I want them to sit on my lap and hear what I achieved through determination and perseverance. But in order to tell those stories, I had to go out and create those stories myself; they didn't just appear for me.

At the end of the day, what you make of your life is up to you. I've always thought "Y-O-U" stands for being "Your Own Usher" through life. You have to guide yourself. By motivating yourself and pursuing the causes that matter to you, you can achieve meaning and true success. No matter how many books you read, in the end, you'll find the best source of inspiration within yourself. Use it to achieve success as an entrepreneur and as a leader; then, give back to your community. Deliver both your packages. Make a difference in someone else's life and, in turn, find satisfaction in yours.

MY FAMILY

Alingon (younger son), Me, Sheema (my wife), Abiskar (older son)

ACKNOWLEDGMENTS

To Scribe, without the team's ongoing support, this book could not be published so soon. Sincere thanks to every one of you who were so friendly and helped me to make it happen.

To Dr. Richard Prager, you are not only a fellow Rotarian but a good friend. You have always been there to help our family. You are an extraordinary photographer. My profound thanks for taking the pictures of me and my family for my book.

To all my clients in America and around the world, I can't find the right words to thank you enough for trusting in our ability, knowledge, and service. Your continued support helped us grow from the basement of my house to a high-rise building in downtown Worcester. It has been a blessing to be able to serve your needs for more than twenty-five years. There would be no entrepreneurship for me without all of you. Million thanks!

To the many community leaders in Worcester who helped me establish my business by giving me the opportunity to be a part of the city. A big thank you, my friends.

To Lynn, who has been a truly dedicated employee in my business for over 25 years. I could not write this book if the business did not reach the heights it has achieved today. Your role has been significant. No words are enough to acknowledge your immense sense of responsibility. You have been someone I could always count on. I thank you from the very core of my heart.

To my late dearest brother (Dada) and late sister-in-law (Boudi) who unselfishly gave me all they could so I could earn my higher education that qualified me to come to America. Your support was priceless! I will always remain indebted to you.

To my beloved sister (Didi), who cared for me like her own son. Her care, love, and emotion were sources of my healing after my mother passed away. Didi, you gave me what I needed the most: "solace." I know how you feel for me. I feel you in my heart. Be there always, Didi.

To my two sons, my true heart beats, Abiskar (Big Guy) and Alingon (Little Guy), two blessed jewels of my life. You two are everything for me! My love, my inspiration, my support, my real courage and strength. This book could not be completed if both of you would not take the ownership to review, revise, and reshape it. So proud of you my sons. My deepest love and hearty blessings will always be for you. I will always remain within you.

To my life's partner, Sheema, without whom I cannot comprehend my life. You are a perfect wife and a loving, caring mother. You understand me and my passion. Your support and sacrifice for me inspire me every day. Without you, I could not achieve anything. The business, the foundation, and this book have all been possible only because you came in my life. You deserve all the applause, credit, kudos and bravos. May god bless us to be with each other on Earth and in heaven!

ABOUT THE AUTHOR

 **DR. SATYA MITRA** is a successful entrepreneur who has dedicated his life to serving others. After earning his PhD from India, he relocated to the United States where he and his wife, Sheema, opened The Guru Tax and Financial Services in Worcester, Massachusetts. They are also the founders of Joy Guru Humanitarian Services, a highly respected nonprofit organization (www.joyguru.org). Dr. Mitra serves on several community boards and has twice been named Rotarian of the Year. He hosts a local radio program and is a popular motivational and leadership speaker (www.drsatyamitra.com).

61706033R00090